W9-AJN-131

That They May Be One in Christ

by

Dr. Cheryl Fortson

Vincom Publishing Co.
Tulsa, Oklahoma

That They May Be One in Christ
ISBN 0-927936-19-4
Copyright © 2000 by
Dr. Cheryl Fortson
42 East Dudley Town Road
Bloomfield, CT 06002

Published by Vincom Publishing Co.
P. O. Box 702400
Tulsa, OK 74170
(918) 254-1276

Dedication

I am so very grateful to be able to dedicate this book to my husband, John, who has been my sweetheart and friend in marriage for thirty-six years. I thank God for giving me such a faithful companion for life, who has covered me in prayer and encouraged me to become "all" that God has created me to be. He has been my number one supporter and is presently serving alongside me in the ministry at Full Gospel. Together we are fulfilling God's divine purpose and plan for our lives.

I would also like to dedicate this book to my three faithful children and their spouses. Each one of them has committed their lives to following Christ and serving along with me in the ministry at Full Gospel. I want to personally thank each one: Minister John Jr. and Doreen, Youth Pastor Darryl and Prophetess Christine, and Chervon and James.

Last, but not least, I also dedicate this book to my twelve precious grandchildren who love the Lord and bring such joy to our lives. Our five grandsons are: Stephen, Kijuan, Keelon, Darryl Jr., and Christopher. Our seven granddaughters are: Cherelle, Ahzja, Shalia, Jasmine, Cheyna, Daysha, and Kiarrah Cherisse. To my Godson, Darryl Jr. and my Goddaughters, Tiffany and Naomi.

Acknowledgements

I want to acknowledge and highly esteem the Lord of my life for choosing me and calling me into the ministry even before the foundation of the world. Thank You for anointing me to release this great revelation that I believe will help to bring "comfort and one-ness" to the Body of Christ.

I also want to thank my faithfully anointed administrator, Prophetess Lisa, who has been with me from the very beginning of the ministry and has continued to believe in me. You have never stopped encouraging me to obey each prophetic voice that has come to release me to write the books that are inside of me.

I would like to acknowledge my powerfully anointed and faithful head intercessor, Elder Deborah, our prophetic intercessory prayer ministry, and our entire Full Gospel covenant family. Because of your faithful commitment to cover me daily with great militant prayer, I have been able to release this apostolic work in a book. I certainly appreciate each of you for allowing me to teach the revelations in this book to you first.

I would like to acknowledge the wonderful people who have prophesied the word of the Lord to me and encouraged me to write my books. I want to thank Bishop Gary McIntosh, Prophet Wayman Thomas, Prophet Lloyd Bustard, Prophet Vivian E. Duncan, and my very good friends from Tulsa, Prophetess Brenda and Tomm Todd, and the ones who are helping to make this book a reality, Prophetess Pam and George Vinnett. I hesed-agape (love) each of you and thank you for being divine connections in my life.

Contents

Foreword by Pam Vinnett

In the twenty-first century, the Church of Jesus Christ will see more tumult and opposition than in any other century that has preceded it. That not withstanding, she shall see her greatest hour of victory if she does not faint. Therefore it is mandatory that we develop the ability to follow in the footsteps of our Lord in every way possible.

That They May Be One in Christ is a pertinent, challenging and timely book, addressing an issue that is so very critical to the Church's survival and ultimate victory: *unity.* Unity covers a wide gamut of needs in virtually any group, particularly the Church, from the necessity to interact properly as leaders with leaders, to peacefully resolve conflicts among the brethren and to develop harmony and togetherness in a household among all members. It is a huge little word with wretched ramifications if disallowed or disobeyed.

Cheryl Fortson lives a life of covenant and unity as the pastor of a thriving, challenging church and as a wife and mother. She is a woman of an excellent reputation that is earned, and thus should be given the respect of one who has learned the value of unification for the purpose of right living. Being tested in ways that few warriors have experienced, this valiant woman has actually found the keys to success in God's Kingdom, and that is to love without favoritism and to keep covenant, charging the expense to the covenant breaker, Satan himself.

I have said many times in ministry that I would not care for one to minister to me who bore no scars from previous battles. A friend describes it this way: You will never have a fragrance until you have been crushed. Cheryl Fortson's fragrance is strong and vibrant and will uplift the soul, for her experiences and triumphs qualify her to speak into the Body with wisdom on this subject.

I am a firm believer in the fact that most Christians find it quite easy to have prejudices and carry grudges for a variety of reasons. The core reason for this is found in a revelation that Jesus shared with me while I was going through a difficult experience with a former ministry laborer. I inquired of God, "How could this happen? How can someone who professes love for me one day become so vicious and vehement the next?" He responded, "This happens because people secretly doubt that I am capable of taking care of them and that I just might not be real. Therefore they take matters into their own hands just when they believe I can't or won't handle it."

The bitter truth is that there is simply not enough observance of covenant love and unity in the Body of Christ for us to complete the work we were sent to do. However, this fact is changeable! We can make the change today if we put in motion the principles espoused in this book. If you feel that women were somehow created less than a male or fell to that estate, you are prejudiced. If you discriminate against people who have not experienced glossolalia (speaking in tongues) and you have, or vice versa, you are prejudiced. If you say you are a Christian and you hate another Christian because of the color of their skin, you are prejudiced. If you feel that all leadership is corrupt because you have experienced corruption in leadership, you are prejudiced. If you are a slanderer and practice gossip, you are prejudiced. The list is endless. **Prejudice is a sin** regardless of what it is directed toward.

The definition of "unity" (oneness) is the fact, quality, or condition of being one, according to Webster. Unity brings life while disunity brings death. This writing is not one to be ignored, but one that must be read, digested and ingested to understand its substance. It will bring great conviction upon the heart that is truly surrendered to Christ, allowing a fresh cleansing by the washing of the water of the Word. Read it. Really read it until you echo its sentiments and cry aloud to the Body of Christ around the world, *That We May Be One in Christ!*

Introduction

My true heart's desire for writing this book is to help to bring a spirit of comfort and unity to the Body of Christ. I believe that the words in this book declare the heart of our Lord when He released His prophetic intercessory prayer for the entire Church in the 17th chapter of the Gospel of Saint John.

Our great High Priest spoke these words in verse 21 just before His triumphant return back to the Father:

> **That they all may be one [just] as You, Father, are in Me and I in You, that they also may be one in Us, so that the world may believe and be convinced that You have sent Me.**

Because Christ Jesus **always** submitted to the divine will of the Father in everything He did while in the earth, I believe what He was praying was the heart and the will of the Father for His Church.

I believe also that the honor and glory that the Lord said He imparted into His Church has given the Church the ability to reflect His image in the earth. He stated that just as the Father and He were "one," we would be "one."

Jesus declared in this 17th chapter of Saint John that He was going to **continue** to reveal the Father's name and character in the earth. The only way that He can effectively do that is through a **united** Body of anointed believers who are one in Christ.

Paul stated in Galatians 3:26-29:

> **In Christ Jesus you are *all sons* of God through faith.**
>
> **For as many [of you] as were baptized into Christ – into a spiritual union and communion with Christ, the Anointed One, the Messiah – have put on (clothed yourselves with) Christ.**

11

There is [now no distinction], neither Jew nor Greek, there is neither slave nor free, there is not male and female; for you are all one in Christ Jesus.

And if you belong to Christ (are in Him, Who is Abraham's Seed), then you are Abraham's offspring and [spiritual] heirs according to promise.

Because the Word of God does not change, this Word is already eternally settled forever, the believer in Christ is clothed in the anointing so there should be *no more racial bias, no more cultural bias and no more gender bias* found among us.

The Body of Christ has been legally purchased by the blood of Jesus and placed back into **our original place** in God before the fall. Both male and female were made in the image and likeness of God and both were given the same equal dominion in the earth. This is why God called them both *Adam*. God has already chosen a specific purpose for each person in the Body, before the foundation of the world.

Not one of us will be able to escape the fact that we will have to stand before our holy God and give an account over that which He sent us out of Himself into the earth to do.

I am forever grateful that I am in relationship with a mate who has recognized the valuable call on my life and has released me to become all that God created me to be in Christ Jesus, our Lord.

I am sorry to say that this will not happen for everyone in the Body of Christ, because of the traditions of men that make the Word of God of none effect! Gender bias will keep many important ministry gifts from being released into their place of purpose.

Through the message in this book, I will continue to remind the Church that it is important that we remember that Christ Jesus has already prayed **"that they *all* may be one."**

We must never forget that God always watches over His Word to perform it! And we should not be ignorant of the fact that our arms are entirely too short to box with God!

Saints of the Most High God, it is time for the Body of Christ, both males and females, to grow up! Get rid of all prejudices and become the militant Church that God expects us to be so the Kingdom of God can be revealed to the kingdoms of this world.

1

Mankind in Christ

They are not of the world, even as I am not of the world. Sanctify them through thy truth: thy word is truth. As thou hast sent me into the world, even so have I also sent them into the world.

John 17:16-18 KJV

Many years ago the Lord began to deal with me about a certain concept in His Word and to reveal a deeper understanding to my spirit — because my mind was not mature enough to grasp everything that He was saying.

What He began to deal with me about was the desire of His heart for the Church, the Body of Christ. His desire was gravely different than what I was seeing with my natural eyes. So much so that sometimes I would get confused about what He was showing me.

However, He continued to feed me divine knowledge and began to perfect me in experience and to draw me closer to Himself. The "bottom line" of every single time He showed me His heart's desire was that the Church would be one as He and the Father are one.

When this book began to take shape out of messages along this line, the Lord gave me this title *That They May Be One in Christ.* Of course, this was not new "revelation" but new understanding for me of what already had been revealed in His Word.

Jesus told His disciples what His desire was for the Church, but somehow we tend to overlook that and focus on Mark 16:15-18. His desire for how His Body, the Church, is to be in its corporate nature is one thing. The commandment concerning what the Church is to do *is an entirely different thing.*

It is like a person: *Who you are* and *what you do* are not the same, although what you do flows out of who you are. Therefore, how can we successfully go and make disciples of all nations *if, as the Body of Christ, we are not truly one in nature as Jesus desires us to be*?

As long as we are divided among races, genders, and social classes, the disciples we make will "inherit" that nature and also be divided!

Certainly, all Christians will not ever believe every little, or even big, doctrine exactly alike with as much human nature as we still have. The only way to have outward unity is by compromising somewhere on things that matter. That will result in the global religion we saw its proponents beginning to put together recently at a huge United Nations conference.

God and the Son were not talking of being one in all our beliefs — in our minds — but being one in spirit, being one in love for one another, one in heart overlooking differences in things that are not spelled out in the Word. However, the basic accepted Christian doctrines such as the Trinity, the Virgin Birth, the death and resurrection of Jesus, and His second coming certainly will be the foundation of our unity.

In John 17, we find Jesus making His "valedictory" message, His final personal words, to the disciples before the crucifixion. In those verses, Jesus summed up His ministry and the legacy He wanted to leave for His followers, those who were to go out and take the gospel to the nations.

As verse 18 at the beginning of this chapter says: **As thou hast sent me . . . even so have I also sent them. . . .**

Notice that what He said in this chapter of John is not for the unsaved, but for those who make up His Body represented at that time by the first disciples. Particularly look at verses 20-23 in *The Amplified Version*, which gives most of the possible meanings and is used for most scriptures in this book.

> **Neither for these alone do I pray — it is not for their sake only that I make this request — but also for all those who will ever come to believe in (trust, cling to, rely on) Me through their word and teaching** (v. 20).

Do you know that everything Jesus prayed came to pass? Why did it come to pass? Because He only prayed what the Father told Him to pray. He only did what He saw the Father do. (John 5:19.)

He did not do anything of His own so, if He prayed it, you had better believe it was already etched in stone!

He was praying for all who would ever come to believe in Him. That is you and me, if we "trust in, cling to, and rely on" Him through our word and teaching. *What did He pray for us?* The answer is in verse 21:

> **So that they all may be one [just] as You, Father, are in Me and I in You, that they also may be one in Us, so that the world may believe and be convinced that You have sent Me.**

Why Should We Be One?

Why should we all be one as He and the Father are one? That is the only way we truly show the world that Jesus is real and that He is sent from God. Only if they see the Church love one another in spite of differences of all kinds will they believe Jesus sent us, and the Father sent Him.

No wonder most of the world does not believe!

All of one race of Christians is not in unity, to say nothing of unity across races!

All male Christians are not in agreement with each other, much less with all female Christians.

All Christians of one nationality are not in unity with all Christians of other nationalities — so no wonder we are not being the light and salt of the world. (Matthew 5:13-16.)

How could Jesus leave these words as His "Last Will and Testament," His legacy to His Body? Let's tie John 17:14 with John 17:22, which is the key:

> **I have given and delivered to them Your Word (message); and the world has hated them, because they are not of the world — do not belong to the world — [just] as I am not of the world** (v. 14). **I have given to them the glory and honor which You have given Me, that they may be one, [even] as We are one** (v. 22).

Jesus was saying, "I have the legal right to do this, because You gave it to Me, Father. I have given to them *the glory*."

Where did the glory come from? It came from the Father.

What is the glory? It is His image, His essence, His nature, His character — everything that makes God Who He is.

Who did He give the glory to? Only Jews? Or Jews and Gentiles (which meant all non-Jews)? Only men? Or men and women?

He gave the glory and honor that was His from the Father to *everyone who believes on Him.*

That is why the Apostle Paul wrote to the Christians at Galatia that we are no more male or female, bond or free, Jew or Greek. (Galatians 3:28.) He wrote along the same lines to the churches at Ephesus (2:11-14):

> **Therefore remember that at one time you were Gentiles [heathen] in the flesh . . . separated (living apart) from Christ — excluded from all part in Him; utterly estranged and outlawed from the rights of Israel as a nation, and strangers with no share in the sacred compacts of the [Messianic] promise — with no knowledge of or right in God's agreements, His covenants. And you had no hope — no promise; you were in the world without God. But now in**

Christ Jesus, you who once were [so] far away **in) the blood of Christ have been brought nea** **[Himself] our peace — our bond of unity and ha** **has made us both [Jew and Gentile] one (body), au** **ken down (destroyed, abolished) the hostile divi** **wall** **between us.**

Christ has broken that wall of hostility down. Man wants to keep the wall intact. Tradition wants to keep it in place. To walk in right standing with the Lord, Christians need to agree with what the Word says. The only way we will ever be all that we are supposed to be in Christ is to believe what the Word says.

Christ took all races and nationalities (Jews and Gentiles, which includes everyone else) and made *one new man* out of them. He did this legally by "abolishing" on the cross the curses and penalties that were still on all races other than the Hebrews/Israelites/Jews.

They had been exempted through the Abrahamic covenant — a "credit card" so to speak — on the full, complete covenant between God and mankind ratified by Jesus on the cross.

And [He designed] to reconcile to God both [Jew and Gentile, united] in a single body by means of His cross; thereby killing the mutual enmity and bringing the feud to an end.

Ephesians 2:16

God said it ended, and we need to accept that. He said peace to the Jew and peace to the Gentile (non-Jew or Israelite). He brought everyone who receives Him together as one, irrespective of differences, making no distinctions.

In the Body, we are equally one. Every Christian has the same access to the one Father through one Head, Jesus our Mediator, and by one Spirit. (Ephesians 2:18.)

We Are No Longer Aliens

Therefore, all non-Israelites who were not part of the Abrahamic covenant are no longer aliens to the Nation of Israel. In addition, through Jesus, all Christians are now also Abraham's seed, adopted by faith through a blood covenant. (Galatians 3:29.)

> **Therefore you are no longer outsiders — exiles, migrants and aliens, excluded from the rights of citizens; but you now share citizenship with the saints — God's own people, consecrated and set apart for Himself; and you belong to God's [own] household.**
>
> **Ephesians 2:19**

Now do you want to tell part of God's house, "You don't belong here"; part of God's house, "You be silent"; part of God's house, "You cannot read the Bible and attend services with another part"?

We need to continue to have that zeal and that excitement about what He has called us to do, and not cower down and back off. We have a right to grow and increase **. . . into a holy temple in the Lord — a sanctuary dedicated, consecrated and sacred to the presence of the Lord** (Ephesians 2:21).

Paul also wrote in First Corinthians 3:16 that we are being built into a dwelling place of and for God. We are a dwelling place, individually and corporately.

> **Do you not discern and understand that you . . . are God's temple (His sanctuary), and that God's Spirit has His permanent dwelling in you — to be at home in you [collectively as a church and also individually]?**

We are all dwelling places of the presence of God. God wants to use each one of us. Anyone who cowers back and does not let God use him or her will keep the Body from growing into the maturity and to its whole fullness.

Everyone is needed. All are sons of God. He made us into "one new man" out of both the Jew and non-Jewish believers. He annulled the rules and regulations of the separations through the law. Every born-again believer is included in His body.

Now let us look at the third category of *pre-Jesus* separations in man: 1) races/nationalities, 2) free man or slave (social/economic classes) and 3) male and female.

> **There is [now no distinction], neither Jew nor Greek, there is neither slave nor free, there is not male and female; for you are all one in Christ Jesus.**

> **Galatians 3:28**

As with anything in the Bible, we need to go back to the beginning and see God's original intent, what things meant when the earth was created. In Bible interpretation, this principle is called "the Law of First Reference."

Others have said that if you do not understand Genesis, you cannot truly understand Revelation, because from beginning to end, God does not change, and His plan flows always forward to culmination.

2

And God Made *Them* Adam

So God created man in his own image, in the image of God he created him; male and female created he them . . . Male and female created he them; and blessed them, and called their name Adam, in the day when they were created.

Genesis 1:27; 5:2 KJV

In the Bible, the Body is referred to as "he," "him," or "man." The female when first created out of the male in the garden was named *wo-man*, or the man with the womb. (Genesis 2:22-24.) Adam called his wife Eve because she became the mother of all living. (Genesis 3:20.)

God looks for oneness. The Father never operated outside of the Son. The Son never operated outside of the Holy Ghost. All three members of the Godhead flow as one. Christ is the Head of the Church, and God considers all of us one in Christ and all of us His witnesses.

The Church cannot have real spiritual power until we all walk as one in Christ.

A husband cannot have real spiritual power unless he walks with his wife in unity, as one. So he will be struggling all his life to accomplish what? A lot of men spend all of their time and energy trying to do something that would be so easy if they truly "hooked up" together with their mates.

The Church is weak because it has rejected part of its potential power. For too many years, women have not been considered

21

part of the "one" Body, but second-class citizens of the Kingdom. A lot of God's Word in the New Testament has been overlooked and brushed aside, and other wrongly interpreted verses have been accepted as "law" because they fit secular tradition.

A long time ago, God began to reveal to me that from the very beginning, He had called both men and women *adam*. However, I did not understand what He meant, having been reared in churches where the traditional interpretation of the woman's role prevailed.

Recently, however, God sent me to the men in my church on an assignment to discuss His desire to bridge the gap between husbands and wives in *this* ministry. The pieces of truth God had shown me over the years began to come together as a whole.

God allowed me to share with our men that His original plan for oneness in His Church would come to pass only when our homes are put in order. Until oneness comes in the home, there will be a gap or an obstacle to hinder oneness taking place in the Church.

Most people now are zeroing in on the racial prejudice gap in the Body of Christ. They really believe that is probably the strongest gap that still exists. There is no question prejudice needs to be addressed so that Christians of all races operate as one. However, God has shown me that is not the greatest gap keeping the Church from unity: *The greatest gap is gender.*

The enemy has a large portion of the Body of Christ blinded. They are fighting over many issues that are not basic to the Church foundation. In the meantime, the enemy is running rampant in marriages, homes, and families and trying every way he can to widen the "gender gap."

The divorce and separation rate is so high because we will not focus in on the heart of God for His people. The Bible tells us that God *called them both adam*. At a recent meeting, I shared with our men God's plan of governmental order in the home for scriptural headship and submission.

Some heard it from me for the first time, but there were others there who had heard it before. However, many in the room were still in grave error. God allowed me to share with them that He was waiting on the heads in the homes to get things in order. Then, He said, order will happen in the Church.

When there is disrespect for one another in the home, there cannot help but be disrespect for one another in our churches. If we have a wrong concept of why God said the male and female must be one in the home, we will certainly have the wrong concept of oneness in the Church for the male and female.

The "gender gap" has been a well put-together scheme and plot of the enemy to keep the Church from growing into full manhood and from becoming one in Him.

True Authority Requires Oneness

Following that meeting in which God did some tremendous work in our men, through one of God's planned "coincidences," an excerpt from a book came into my hands.[1] The title for this chapter is one I borrowed from that article, which started to bring all of the "bits and pieces" God had given me on this subject together as solid truth.

Then God sent me to the book of Genesis to do some extensive word study on the subject of His original plan for mankind. I began to be led by the Spirit to study Genesis 1:26-31 in depth. He began to show me things as I had never seen them before.

According to Genesis 1:26,27, God created man in His own image. Why would He say created *him*, and then add *male and female* if male and female were separate? Him, or *adam*, or man, is to God one being, male and female.

Adam is a Hebrew word meaning "a human being (an individual or the species, mankind, etc."[2] We have turned it into meaning only a proper name, the name of the first man. However, *adam* means mankind. Every time you see the word, it is not referring *only* to the "male man" Adam. Mankind is male and female.

There are many different translations for the word *man*, and you must go back to the original Hebrew and Greek to know whether each word means man as a male generically, a man specifically, or mankind, male and female collectively.

In Genesis 1, the Lord was talking about both male and female, using the word *man* and the word *him*, translated as the Hebrew *adam*. Those verses refer to generic man as the image of God, the crown of His creation distinct from the rest of creation.

When God said, **Let us make man in our image,** he meant mankind was to be different from all other creations. Also, whether male or female, both were made in His image and in His likeness and both were given leadership qualities of dominion.

The "dominion" verse in which God set down clearly that man was to be in authority, or a steward, or a ruler for God, over the rest of creation is Genesis 1:28. In it, God blessed *them*, not just "him," and gave *them* the dominion commandment: be fruitful, multiply, replenish the earth and subdue it, and have dominion over all other living things.

If God had intended the female *adam* to be of lesser value and in lesser authority, He would have limited *them* to being fruitful and multiplying and spoke the rest of that verse only to *him*, the male. However, He did not. He extended the instructions for both male and female to replenish and subdue the earth and have dominion.

Man was distinct from the rest of creation. God put the male and female equally in a place of honor. In essence, He said they are created "after Our image and Our likeness" and have complete authority.

In the previous chapter, we read in John 17 where Jesus said, "I have given them the same honor and glory, Father, that You have given Me."

Again, to whom does *them* refer? Jesus was saying that all those, irrespective of gender, who believe and trust in Him will receive the same amount of honor and glory. God had great plans for male and female man to operate together as one. Even after the fall, in which the first couple forfeited dominion to Satan, God still used the Word *adam* to denote mankind as both genders.

We see this in First Corinthians 15:45-49, where Paul wrote that Jesus is "the Second Man," who through His crucifixion restored male and female to their original place of oneness in Him by tearing down the wall of hostility between the genders.

However, since early days, the Church has been fighting that fact. Actually, the Church traditionally has fought the fact that the wall was torn down between races and classes, as well. Many Christians who still have gender, race, or social biases would like those verses in Galatians and Ephesians not to be in the Book!

God only sees two "men" in all creation:

1. The first man, *adam*, who was created male and female, and in whom were all human beings since then. In Adam and Eve, we are born "one" collectively.

2. The Second Man, Jesus, God's *only begotten* Son, the first-born of many brethren. (Romans 8:29.) In Him, all of the many brethren (male and female) are being restored as "one being," or one man (male and female).

The descendants of Adam who receive Jesus as Savior become one with one another and with Jesus, the Head, through adoption by the blood covenant ratified by Jesus on the cross. (Romans 8:15; Ephesians 1:5.) Galatians 4:5 says *we* (male and female) received the *adoption of sons*. Romans 8:23 says that when our bodies are resurrected, our manifestation as God's sons (male and female) will be revealed.

The problem is that, although we are all joined as one in the spirit positionally, we certainly do not act as one in the natural. Nor are our hearts joined as one. We behave as if the "wall of hostility" still exists. We live in spiritual unreality, spiritual deception, and believe a spiritual falsehood.

The greatest error and the root cause of division, however, is in our homes. There is no oneness in many homes. The enemy works very early in most of our lives to make women feel inferior and men to feel superior.

The moment any woman begins to discover her authority in God, she often is branded as operating in a "Jezebel spirit." When a woman moves into her place called of God, however, it is because she is made in the image and likeness of God.

Many women have been crushed and their ministries aborted because they have been treated as "Jezebelic" and out of order. God has shown me, however, that the only way the Bible can be fulfilled and the Church come to full manhood is when oneness is truly achieved.

Jesus was praying in John 17, "Father, I want the original plan restored. Just as they see Us operating as one, it is time for them (male and female) to operate as one."

Expect Warfare Before This Happens

Those of us preaching this level of oneness can expect to find ourselves in a real war. However, we are responsible to speak it forth from now on, because truth has been revealed to us. Anytime God sends you to bring correction to grave error, you are going to have your hands full. Many people will not like you.

Anything on which a husband and wife agree cannot be stopped by the devil — hindered temporarily sometimes, but not defeated. Can you imagine then, a time when the Church becomes one? Anything on which we agree cannot be stopped. However, what if the enemy can keep us divided?

God instructed man (male and female) to subdue the earth, using all its vast resources in the service of God and man. He gave us the authority, and Jesus restored it when He defeated Satan on the cross. (Colossians 2:14.)

God said, "And have dominion." He said *have* it, but have dominion over what? We are to have dominion over **. . . the fish of the sea, the birds of the air, and over every living creature that moves upon the earth** (Genesis 1:28).

God blessed them both, male and female *adam*, and He gave both His favor equally, and said to both, "You have dominion together." The Hebrew word *radah* translated *dominion* means "to subjugate, to prevail against, to reign or rule (over)."[3]

God did not mean *adam* to rule separately but together as one. He did not give one the authority to rule and the other one not.

Be fruitful together, multiply together, subdue and replenish together as one, and have dominion together as one. Be released as one in Me, God was saying.

He released male and female *adam* as one to walk in His power of attorney and authority in the earth. When we walk in one-ness we have the power of attorney and the authority once again through the Second Man, Jesus. That gives us the ability to get anything done that God sends us to do. The power is released in the oneness.

Within the oneness, of course, there are levels of authority, different areas of responsibility. This is not a book about the fivefold offices. However, briefly, each office has its own level of authority and realm of responsibility.

A layman does not have the authority within the Body of someone set in a fivefold office, even if many Charismatics think they do. What we are dealing with is two separate things: 1) equality of genders, races and nationalities, and social classes (free and slave in Jesus' day) before God; and 2) authority levels in the Church, in the home, in civil government, and so forth.

The point is that anyone from the first group can be called by God to fill any position in the second group. There are distinctions in the Bible in authority levels within the Body of Christ, *but there are no distinctions in the Bible between the three categories in the first group.*

In other words, any man or woman, anyone of any race or nation, and anyone of any social class can be called as pastor, teacher, evangelist, prophet, or apostle — and have equal "dominion" over whatever area God gives them.

As a bottom-line example: A poverty-stricken, black woman can be called of God as an apostle. Some Christians have accepted that women can be pastors, but would balk at a woman apostle. Again, this book does not have the scope to discuss the "proofs" from the Bible to this effect. Other authors have done this, although not many. I can recommend a couple of very good books along this line.[4]

[1]Pickett, Dr. Fuchsia T. *God's Dream* (Orlando, FL: Creation House), excerpted under the title "And God Made Them Adam" in *Dimensions*, a former newsletter of Higher Dimension Church and Ministries, Tulsa, OK, Vol. 2, Issue 2, pp. 60,61.

[2]Strong, James. *The New Strong's Exhaustive Concordance of the Bible*, Comfort Print Edition, (Nashville, TN: Thomas Nelson Publishers, 1995), "New Strong's Concise Dictionary of the Words in the Hebrew Bible," p. 3, #120.

[3]Ibid, p. 130, #7287.

[4]Trombley, Charles. *Who Said Women Can't Teach*, (South Plainfield, NJ: Bridge Publishing Co., 1985), and Vinnett, Pam. *For Women Only*, (Tulsa, OK: Vincom Publishing Co., 1998).

3

Love and Respect

Husbands, love your wives, as Christ loved the church and gave Himself up for her . . . Even so husbands should love their wives as [being in a sense] their own bodies. *He who loves his own wife loves himself.*

Ephesians 5:25,28

For centuries, the Church has ignored the fact that male and female were to have dominion as one over the world (Genesis 1:28) and in the Church or the Kingdom. (Galatians 3:28.) However, it is confusion not to realize that there are levels of authority — which is different from equality of dominion — governed by church office, civil office, and God's order in the family.

The male was given the responsibility to protect and make final decisions in the family, as the pastor is in the church. When husband and wife are truly one, or at least operating in agreement, then there is no conflict, no strife and contention.

Children are to obey the parents, and the parents should agree on family rules, and so forth. When parents are not one, then confusion prevails, order is topsy-turvy, and children rule instead of parents. Unfortunately, in too many households today, that is the way it is.

As scriptural heads of their homes, men (male *adams*) are the Lord's servants. Ephesians 5:23 says that the husband is "head" of the wife as Jesus is "head" of the Church. *The Bible nowhere says that all men are "heads" over all women!* However, that is the religious tradition: All men are somehow a rank in God higher than all women.

God placed the male "man" in the house to minister and to tend. Under the New Covenant, we find that as leaders in the home, husbands are to be examples of Christ. (Ephesians 5:23-33.)

Also, scriptural headship means they are called by God to be the lovers. The world has corrupted many men's minds through pornography and even the general media into thinking that women are to pursue them. Many men do not even know they have perverted minds, because what they believe seems like the norm.

Husbands are to be stewards over their families — answerable to God for the responsibility — the providers, and trustees over their families. That may seem like such a heavy responsibility that the enemy has fooled some men into thinking they cannot do it. God would never call you to do something He did not equip you to do.

Notice that God admonished men to *love* their wives several times, but only once are wives told to love their husbands. (Titus 2:4.) That is because most wives do that without being told! Men too many time equate "love" with "sex" and do not care about their wives as much as their own bodies.

On the other hand, what wives are reminded to do several times is to *respect and reverence* their husbands. In the process of equality being restored to women, the enemy has gotten involved and pushed that move of God to the extreme. Now we have women taking headship, women even being contemptuous and putting down men, and even God Himself portrayed as an "old meanie" out to keep women downtrodden.

> **. . . And let the wife see that she respects and reverences her husband — that she notices him, regards him, honors him, prefers him, venerates and esteems him; and that she defers to him, praises him, and loves and admires him exceedingly.**
>
> **Ephesians 5:33**

How many Christian wives do this? Many will say, "But he does this or that," or "but he is this way or that way." Paul, writing under inspiration of the Holy Spirit, makes no exceptions.

Of course, not all husbands are perfect in living up to their roles. Neither is every President of the United States.

However, *because of the office*, when a president appears in public or even is approached privately by those outside his family, he is treated respectfully. He is given the reverence due his office.

Wives, if your husbands are not perfect, begin to give them the respect due the office and see what happens. Get your own attitude in order, and let God handle your husband's shortcomings. You are not his Holy Spirit, nor are you accountable to God for his actions and attitudes, only your own.

When God commanded *adam* to be fruitful and multiply, He was not just referring to sex and reproduction. Sex is not the only purpose for a husband and wife coming together. That is why some of us have been so disappointed. Subduing should be going on. Having dominion should be going on today. However, nothing can happen beyond sex, if there is not oneness, because God said for *both of them together to have dominion*.

What Did God Approve in Creation?

The Bible lets us know God rested on the seventh day because everything was done. (Genesis 1:31, 2:2.) He approved His creation completely. He then gave His complete approval of His arrangement and declared forever that it was very good. What was He declaring?

He was approving the "oneness and dominion" that He had decreed. Genesis 1:31 closes out the six days of creation. God saw *everything He had made*, called it good (suitable and pleasant), and *approved it completely*. Moses, who is thought to have written Genesis, was not talking about a different subject in verse 31.

He wrote that God thought the oneness and dominion of *adam* — male and female together — was good, suitable, and pleasant. He *approved it completely*. Guess what, it is still very good today. When a spiritually mature woman and man are one flesh together, God has a force in the earth. There will be no competitive jealousy but a team complementing and celebrating one another's gifts and abilities.

As oneness is in Heaven, it can now be in the earth through Jesus. Look at Genesis 2:7:

> **Then the Lord God formed man** *(adam)* **of the dust of the ground, and breathed into his nostrils the breath or spirit of life; and man** (adam) **became a living being.**

There is something very, very significant in that verse which the Lord showed me. He only went to the earth one time. He only breathed in man's nostrils one time, and all of mankind became living souls inside of Adam at one time. So it was all of mankind that He was breathing into. Now look at verse 18.

> **Now the Lord God said, It is not good [sufficient, satisfactory] that the man should be alone; I will make him a helper meet (suitable, adapted, completing) for him.**

The word *man* in that verse also is "adam," which means that all of mankind should not be alone, and the word *alone* is the Hebrew word *monos*, which means "single or solitary."[1]

The first cause of most misunderstandings concerning what the Bible says comes from reading only one translation and not comparing it with others.

The second cause stems from not studying with a good concordance handy in which to look up the original words and their meanings.

The third cause of misinterpretations and the forming of wrong doctrines is from not studying history, church and secular, to see what the cultural environment was when certain things were written.

John 3:16, for example, fits all cultures and can only be read one way: *Ye must be born again.* (Even then, reincarnation perverts the meaning.) However, the sayings of Paul about women and marriage were instigated by the cultural settings of Jews and Greeks in which women were regarded entirely different.

If you do not know what those settings were and do not understand whether Paul was addressing Jews or Greeks, then you can misinterpret his advice completely.

When God saw it would not be good for *adam* to be alone, He set about constructing a helper for him that would be suitable and would complement the kind of person he was.

He had already started male and female off as one. We were not separate from the beginning. Why are we trying to separate ourselves now and say one part is less than the other?

God Only Created One

God put everything in *adam* (male and female joined) at one time, and then He said, "Now I'm going in and separate *adam* for a purpose."

Look at how He did that in Genesis 2:21,22:

And the Lord God caused a deep sleep to fall on Adam, and while he slept He took one of his ribs — a part of his side — and closed up the [place with] flesh instead of it; and the rib or part of his side which the Lord God had taken from the man, He built up and made into a woman and brought her to the man.

God did not go back to the dust of the earth to start over and make *two* separate beings! He began with *oneness*, then took part of *oneness* and made it into a separate gender, not a separate creation. Notice what Adam said in verse 23 when God brought the woman to him:

Then Adam said, This [creature] is now bone of my bones and flesh of my flesh. She shall be called Woman, because she was taken out of a man.

Sometimes *adam* is used to denote "mankind"; sometimes it evolved into a proper name for the male part of the being created in God's image; sometimes it is used to contrast between the human species and animals. You have to study the context to know which one is meant.

I am stressing this point over and over, because you cannot assume when you see the word *man* in the Bible that it refers only to males. Why did God do it like that? I believe it is because He never saw any difference. He made male and female one being created in His image and likeness, and gave them both dominion *before separating them into genders*.

Later, you will find two different Hebrew words than *adam* used for man and woman, words that cannot be used interchangeably with *adam*. If you read the Bible without knowing these distinctions, you will misinterpret the Word. That is how the enemy can bring division.

People can teach things as doctrine that God did not say when they do not care enough or take the time to study out the original languages. The first popular version of the Bible, *The King James Version*, does not make careful distinctions in many cases.

Those translators had two main problems: They did not have access to some of the original manuscripts we have today, and they used what is known today as "Elizabethan English." Even English words of 400 years ago do not always mean now what they did then — much less always translating exactly what the Hebrew or Greek words meant.

The two Hebrew words that came into use after *adam* and which *always* mean a man or a woman, not mankind or one being, are *iysh* and *ishshah*. God had me look at the original words, translated "man" in verses 21-23 specifically, to see what He was really saying.

Iysh (pronounced "ish") means only "a man, a male, a fellow, a footman, a husband," and so forth. It is never a generic term for man, meaning male and female. You will first find it used in verse 23 when it says "she was taken out of man (*iysh*)."[2]

For the first time, male and female are referred to as separate genders.

The female or feminine version of *ish* is *ishshah*, first used in verse 22, when it says God **made he a woman** (KJV). Again, that is when the *adam* was separated into genders. As we have seen, in mankind's original creation, all *adams*, whether male or female, were given dominion over the rest of God's creation.

You will not find in Scripture anywhere that God made a distinction in that kind of authority between men and women. As one, they were to rule and reign for Him as stewards over His handiwork.

The male and female distinctions do not matter within the Kingdom of God, but they do matter *within* marriage, and God got to that next in verse 24.

> **Therefore a man** (an *adam* of the male gender, *iysh*) **shall leave his father and his mother and shall become united and cleave to his wife** (an *adam* of the female gender, *ishshah*)**, and they shall become one flesh** (as Adam and Eve were in the beginning).

First, God showed us that men and women are both *adam* and both *as one* have dominion and authority over His works on earth.

Second, God separated *adam* into male and female for a purpose.

Third, He told us what the purpose was: that they could work together to fulfill His assignment (Genesis 1:27) by once again and voluntarily loving Him and each other and *becoming one flesh* by choice.

Did God Really Say?

Church, we have missed it, and we have hindered the work and the move of God. Men and women, we have been lied to by the enemy working through false interpretations of God's Word. He never has any new tactics, so he has said to us down through the years, "Did God really say? Was that what God really meant?" (Genesis 3:1.)

One reason so many women are frustrated and "act so ugly" is because the image of God in them is trying to come out, but they are constantly being told that is wrong.

One reason so many men are "macho" and run over their wives is because they have believed the lie that women are second-class people. They believe being the head of the house means throwing their weight around and being tyrants. Many have totally missed the fact that the first commandment to a husband is *to love*, not to rule.

God sent me to the men in our church to say, "You must ask the Holy Spirit to show you specifically what your wife's needs are."

When our homes get right, our churches will get right. Leaders will not be chosen by gender, but by God's selection of those with giftings. Whether our leaders or fivefold offices are male or female will not even enter into the equation.

Husbands and wives must learn that being truly married means being one another's best friend. The Bible asks us, **Can two walk together, except they be agreed?** (Amos 3:3 KJV).

[1]Vine, W. E.; Unger, Merrill F.; White, William Jr. *Vine's Complete Expository Dictionary*, (Nashville: Thomas Nelson Publishers, 1984, 1996), p. 23.

[2]Strong's, "Hebrew Dictionary," p. 7, #376.

4

Who Is Your Best Friend?

For this reason a man shall leave his father and his mother and shall be joined to his wife, and the two shall become one flesh.

Ephesians 5:31

God said in this 24th verse of Genesis, chapter 2, that a husband was to *leave*, be separated from, his parents and unite and cleave to his wife. This is an example of how the English language has changed since the *King James Version* was translated in 1611.

Today, the first and most common definition of *cleave* is "to cut apart" usually with one blow, which is where we get our word "meatcleaver."[1] The second dictionary definition is used today nowhere except in the Bible, and it means exactly the opposite: "to adhere to, to cling to, to be faithful to."[2]

Cleave in the second meaning was a translation of the Hebrew word *dabaq*, meaning "to cling or adhere to, to catch by pursuit in a figurative use, to follow close (hard after), to be joined (together)," and in a variation, *debeq*, meaning "a joint, or by implication, to solder."[3]

I believe God is saying it is now time for husbands and wives to be glued, or soldered, together and to become best friends. If your husband or your wife is not your best friend, you are in grave error with God.

You have to choose to allow this to happen and even make it happen, because you want to obey God, if for no other reason. I did not say wives cannot have girlfriends or husbands menfriends. However, those friends should not be closer to you than your wife or husband.

You cannot cleave to someone else. You are told by God to cleave to your mate. The Bible says a man will leave his mother and father and be glued to his wife. It means to accompany one another. That means where one goes, the other goes.

Husbands will say, "No, I can't be with my wife all the time. Other men will think there is something wrong with me!"

Would you rather have God *know* something is wrong with you? You need to check out your masculinity as well as your spiritual maturity. A truly masculine Christian does not care what anyone else thinks, if he is doing what God said to do.

When you get to know who you are *in Christ*, you will have the correct word to give to those men who would say something smart to you. You will be able to explain that you are obeying God's Word and that your marriage is the most important thing in your life, next to Him.

However, I do not mean guys cannot ever go out for an evening with guys or a wife with her girlfriends. What I am saying that God intended for husbands and wives to do most things together as best friends, to share confidences, and to be truly intimate, not just in bed.

Cleave means to join oneself to one another in spirit, and you seal that or consummate it with a sexual relationship, becoming one flesh.

Today's climate of promiscuity and perverse sex is why so many marriages do not last. If you have sex with someone, becoming one, and then either of you walks away, there are "soul ties" left behind. All those soul ties are following you all the rest of your life — to say nothing of guilt and shame — unless you repent and ask God to cut you loose from them.

Cleave also means to follow closely. How in the world are you going to follow closely if one is over here, and one is over there, if one is sleeping in one room and one in another room? The devil is a liar.

God is going to hold husbands responsible for the marriages, because they were given the headship. There is nothing a wife can do to keep her husband from cleaving to her if he follows the order of God. So, husband, stop putting the blame on your wife. She is not to "set the tone" of the marriage, you are.

Cleave means you are yoked together. How do you yoke two oxen together? Does one get out in front of the other one? No, they walk side by side. They work together; they make things work together; they are a team. It is time for husbands and wives to be teams.

Whether you like it or not, when God called one, He called the other. One may preach and the other not, but the one not preaching had better understand he or she is cleaving with the one who is preaching.

How Do You Walk Yoked Together?

You are not called by God to be yoked up with another man or woman. Husbands and wives should be so close that they start to think alike because they are one. Have you ever seen a couple married fifty years or more who even have grown to look alike? It happens where there is a real closeness.

When one ox in a team limps, does the other not know it? Does it not affect the other's gait as well?

When one ox lies down, can the other continue to stand?

There will be no surprises if you are truly yoked together, because you already know intimately where the other is "walking" or what the other is feeling. You can minister to one another because you know what is hurting the other one.

It does not make sense, and is out of order biblically, for a wife to be sick and a husband not know it unless she tells him. He ought to feel something in his spirit, because part of him is hurting, part of him has a problem. And he will not leave that part of him sick.

Paul wrote in Ephesians 5:29:

For no man ever hated his own flesh, but nourishes and carefully protects and cherishes it, as *Christ does the church.*

That is why the husband is to treat the wife as he does his own body because she is the same to him as his body! How can you not know when your body is hurting?

This is not taught rightly in most of our churches. Instead we have men "lording" it over their wives and acting like a king "whose home is his castle." *Cleaving* together as one is not taught in our pre-marriage counseling sessions. That is why there is no oneness in many marriages.

Many Christians have married for the wrong reasons, not because God put them together but for social or business reasons, for security (someone providing for you or someone taking care of your house) reasons, for I-am-pregnant-and-you-have-to-marry-me reasons, or for lust reasons.

Then they find that any of those reasons is not enough if there is no companionship and you find you really do not like that person. Do you know you can be married to someone you do not like? You can even have a sexual desire for someone you do not like.

Talk about a miserable life! Unfortunately, a lot of folks have, and will, spend the rest of their lives with someone they do not like. Can you imagine a more awful life than to be yoked closely with an "ox" you do not like?

The Apostle Peter also had a few things to say about marriage and husbands and wives:

In the same way you married men should live considerately with [your wives], with an intelligent recognition [of

the marriage relation], honoring the woman as [physically] the weaker, but [realizing that you] are joint heirs of the grace (God's unmerited favor) of life, in order that your prayers may not be hindered and cut off. — Otherwise you cannot pray effectively.

1 Peter 3:7

Peter made several points in that verse:

1. "In the same way" — the same way as what? In the same way Abraham lived with Sarah, and that was *considerately*, with the husband serving the wife's needs before his own. (v. 6.)

2. Women are (usually) physically weaker and need protecting, according to *The Amplified Version* and in the understanding of many. However, some interpret it this way: Men are as strong, thick pottery dishes, and women as fine crystal, which is weaker, more fragile, and will break easier.

3. Knowing that, *in Christ*, you are "joint-heirs" and equal in the Kingdom. By inference, Peter was saying, "Do not act as if your marriage headship gives you headship rights in the Kingdom. Both husband and wife have the same Head, equally, and that is Jesus."

Why did he give men these admonitions? He instructed men in this way for the most important reason we could have: *so our prayers will be answered.* Nowhere will you find that women are responsible for unity with husbands nor for being in agreement as one flesh. That is the responsibility of the marriage head.

The fourth point Peter made was to have "an intelligent recognition" of the marriage relationship. What does that mean?

What Is "an Intelligent Recognition"?

Having "an intelligent recognition of your marriage relation" means husbands should make a point of studying the Word of God to see what the marriage relationship really entails. Husbands also should throw out any traditional and erroneous thinking about wives being almost slaves and husbands rulers.

A wife is to be submissive — loving, kind, and putting the husband ahead of the children, her house, and her job. (1 Peter 3:1-6.) However, that does not mean being a doormat or a slave to her husband.

Having "an intelligent recognition" also means knowing Christ is the Head of your marriage, and He will tell you what to do about any problems. In fact, He will tell you the problems, if you ask Him! You will not even need to go ask Pastor what is the matter with your wife. God will tell you.

The Holy Ghost knows why she acts the way she does. He knows better than anyone because He has been with her. An *intelligent recognition* means "clear and exact knowledge." You should know at all times where your wife is mentally, spiritually, and physically.

Some husbands do not even know their wives are on their way out. Sometimes a wife is still physically in the house but inwardly gone away from her husband.

He might still be walking around saying, "I'm happily married."

She has already checked out on him, and he does not know it, because she has not physically left. She is still in the house for various reasons, perhaps for the sake of the children, perhaps because she thinks she cannot make it outside of the home. However, she has already checked out, and because she has checked out, your prayers are hindered.

If you tamper with the oneness in marriage, it is just like us with Jesus. If we tamper with our oneness with Jesus, we do not get the benefits. What makes us think we can tamper with the oneness in the marital relationship and still get the benefits?

He likens the marriage relationship to the Church. God expects the same thing from husbands that He expects out of Jesus to the Church. No less. Yet the devil has fooled men into thinking they can neglect their wives and even let them walk off, or the husbands can walk off, and it is going to be all right. However, God is going to hold husbands accountable for stewardship. That is the sad part.

God is placing responsibility where it belongs. What was Peter saying? He said very plainly that, if you do not get to know your wife by clear knowledge, your prayers will be cut off. Ignore her if you want to. Go ahead, say it is not your responsibility but hers to make things work. What you say, husband, does not make it so — what God says is what counts.

I wrote in a previous chapter about finding an article on the subject of God making *adam* male and female. When I saw that I almost "flipped out," because God had spoken to me so much for so many years on this subject. Yet, somehow even after talking to the men in my church on some of these things, I still could not get clarity.

After reading the chapter out of Dr. Fuchsia Pickett's book, *God's Dream*, I began to see that, yes, God held both the male and the female responsible. How could He give them both dominion and hold only one accountable? Dr. Pickett wrote:

> There was nothing to which Jesus laid the ax more violently than the traditions of men. There was absolutely nothing that Jesus felt, dealt with more violently when He walked the earth. When it says, "lay the ax," He dealt tremendously with the traditions of men. Because of bondage to tradition, some cannot understand there is no difference between male and female in God's eyes. For "they have not come to faith." Paul declares that when we "come to faith" we will understand there is neither Greek nor barbarian nor male nor female. (Galatians 3:28.)[4]

Dr. Pickett, a well-known author, prophet, and founder of Shekinah Ministries, Blountville, Tennessee, was saying that the reason some believe there is a difference in male and female in the Body of Christ is because they have not come to faith. Paul continued:

> **But now that the faith has come, we are no longer under a trainer — the guardian of our childhood. For in Christ Jesus you are all sons of God through faith. For as many [of you] as were baptized into Christ . . . have put on (clothed yourselves with) Christ. *There is [now no distinction]*, neither Jew nor Greek, there is neither slave nor free, there is not male and female; for you are all one in Christ Jesus.**
>
> **Galatians 3:25-28**

Now that faith has come, we are all, *male and female*, sons of God through faith. So people who have not yet "come of faith" cannot grasp that when Paul said, or when we say, "sons of God," it is irrespective of gender. They are still operating in tradition, not the Word.

People are now starting to attack the race issue, which is a point of division that should be dealt with. They have "come to faith" in the reality of that first clause. However, why have they stopped there? Why do they still think there is a difference in the Body of Christ between male and female?

Those people have finally recognized, "Oh, if we are going to be complete as a Church, we must come together. Whites and blacks and all other races must come together in oneness."

What about the rest of that verse? If we are going to be complete, male and female have got to come together as well.

You cannot teach part of the verse or try to bring to fruition part of the verse and leave out the rest. You cannot attack the race issue and ignore the gender difference and still be spiritually honest.

For too long the devil has told the male *adams* that the pulpit belongs to them and that female *adams* should sit out in the audience, preside at bake sales, give their tithes, and keep their mouths shut.

For those who attend churches with women pastors, do you know how to answer criticism?

When someone asks you how you can follow a woman pastor, tell them you are not following a "woman pastor" because there is neither male nor female in the Kingdom of God, the Body of Christ. You are following the Holy Spirit and the gifting of God no matter which gender He calls to lead your congregation.

In those cases, the pastor has a woman's body, but she is made in God's image just like male pastors. She has been called to a purpose and has an anointing to do the work of God, and that is what matters.

Of course, the biggest ammunition critics of women in ministry bring up are some of the writings of Paul. Is it not odd, however, that they interpret some of his remarks to mean women are not equal in the Church yet totally ignore Galatians 3:28, where Paul specifically states there is no difference between males and females?

Was Paul schizophrenic?

Was he double-minded where women are concerned?

Was he a misogynist, a woman-hater?

Or, is it possible there is an answer — such as that we have misinterpreted his writings?

[1]*Webster's New World Dictionary of American English*, Third College Edition, (New York: Macmillan General Reference, a Prentice Hall/Macmillan Company, 1994, 1991, 1988), p. 260.

[2]Ibid, p. 261.

[3]Strong's "Hebrew Dictionary," p. 30, #'s 1692, 1694

[4]Pickett.

5

What Was Wrong with Paul?

And afterward I will pour out My Spirit upon *all* flesh, and your sons *and your daughters* shall prophesy. . . . Even upon the menservants and *upon the maidservants* in those days will I pour out My Spirit.

Joel 2:28,29

How could Paul write for all women in all public situations to keep quiet and then contradict himself by saying there is no male or female in Christ (the Church or the Kingdom of God)? Something is very wrong with Paul or with the interpretations.

Also, if something is wrong with Paul, why would you follow someone like that? How could you believe what else he wrote? What about Peter, one of the apostles and founders of the Church? (Ephesians 2:20.) He said on the Day of Pentecost that Joel's prophecy had come to pass.

What *was* that prophecy? It was that the Spirit of God was going to come upon our *sons* and *daughters*, our *men*servants and *maid*servants. (Joel 2:28,29.)

Some may say, "Yes, but that was a prophecy for the Israelites living in the southern kingdom of Judah."

That is not the way Peter got it from the Holy Spirit at Pentecost. Peter told the crowd:

But [instead,] this is [the beginning of] what was spoken through the prophet Joel: And it shall come to pass in the last days, God declares, that I will pour out of My Spirit

47

upon all mankind, and your sons and your daughters shall prophesy — telling forth the divine counsels. . . . Yes, and on My menservants also and on My maidservants in those days I will pour out of My Spirit, and they shall prophesy — telling forth the divine counsels and predicting future events pertaining especially to God's kingdom.

Acts 2:16-18

Notice God said His Spirit would be poured forth on all mankind (no distinction in race or nationality, no favoring one over another), and on His *male and female* servants. Also, the word *prophesy* is divided into two meanings in those verses:

1.   Telling forth the divine counsels (preaching,proclaiming the gospel); and

2.   Predicting future events pertaining to the Kingdom, which is the only way we define prophesy today.

In the Old Testament, "prophets" who foretold the future were called "seers." Prophesying could simply be what we would call preaching.

I am sure that some of my readers are already saying, *"But what about* First Corinthians 14:34 where Paul said for women to be silent in church?"

If you study the cultural context and the subject Paul was really addressing, you will see that he was not laying down a general, all-purpose rule to be used everywhere in all circumstances.

The Apostle Paul was not addressing "the woman question" but the "order-in-church-services" question. Corinth was a mixed-race congregation, made up in the majority of Greeks. Many of those women had been converted from temple attendants, whose dress, behavior, and freedom in public were quite different from the Jewish culture.

Jewish women were rarely to even be seen in public, much less speak in a public place, so Paul could not have been talking to them.[1] One reason the ministry of Jesus was so revolutionary is that He counted women among His followers, although not among the primary twelve disciples. That would have gotten Him stoned before He could even get to the cross!

Greek women had no inhibitions about speaking up in public. Apparently, they were babbling away in tongues out of order, with no interpretations, and yelling back and forth asking questions of their husbands. In general, many apparently were making the services chaotic.[2]

Let me give you another excerpt from Dr. Pickett's article:

Paul declared that when we come to faith, we will understand that there is neither Greek nor barbarian nor male nor female, but we are all one in Christ Jesus. God is preparing men and women alike to be filled with the Spirit in the fullness of time and is delivering us from tradition, prejudice, culture, and denominationalism.

We have tried to lay a guilt trip on men by telling them that they are to fulfill every desire and deepest need of a woman. Men have been put into bondage by the expectation of their wives to meet every need of their lives. Though husbands should meet the physical and emotional needs of their wives, they cannot be expected to meet their spiritual needs. That is not God's divine order.

Both men and women are to walk together as one and let God fulfill the cry of their spirits for a true bridegroom. Your husband cannot be your bridegroom spiritually.[3]

Be Subject to One Another

Many men have been gloriously delivered from the burden that some marriage counselors have put upon them to meet their wives' every need. That was not God's intention. God ordained that men and women shall walk with Him and be one, and He would meet both of their innermost needs.

Divine order is higher than the plight of fallen man. It is far more liberating to men and women than having to live under the doctrine of the curse of a fallen Adam and a fallen Eve.

We have been redeemed to be one flesh in Him. We have been bought with a price so that husbands and wives can truly become one. Paul admonishes us to submit ourselves one to another in the fear of God.

God did not mean to put one gender of mankind over another. He intended for them to walk together as one, submitting themselves one to another. Most traditionalists where men and women are concerned love to start with Ephesians 5:22 where Paul wrote for wives to submit to their husbands.

However, they skip over the previous verse where Paul wrote for everyone in the Church, male or female, to *be subject to one another*. What reason did he give for this advice? It was in order to show reverence for Christ, to show that we are one as He and the Father are one.

Then he wrote, in the same context of showing reverence for Christ, how husbands and wives should treat one another. He used a right marriage as a picture, or an illustration, of the Church and Jesus. He was not specifically setting out to delineate marriage relationships.

He wanted us to see the love of Jesus for us and what our proper attitudes should be to Him and to each other as members of the same Body. In another place, he did the same thing by using members of our physical bodies compared to members of "one Body," the Church. (Ephesians 4:4.)

This understanding does not destroy the order of the home. It does not touch delegated authority. It does not make women higher than men or make them aggressive or domineering. It puts man and woman back together in Jesus.

We do not need "Women's Lib" or ERA. Those women are only trying to get even with men by becoming rulers over them or doing without men. That is as much a perversion of God's plan of male and female joined as one as the traditional pattern of male over female has been.

I want to be redeemed to God's purpose for mankind, to become who I was made to be in God and walk beside the man with whom I am supposed to walk. In Christ, there is to be neither male nor female, but mankind walking together.

Again, the theme God gave me for this book is "Women: Be Free," because He created male and female as one *adam*. Therefore, all of Paul's teachings on women and marriage cannot be dealt with in depth. However, briefly, let me try to summarize his real teachings.

What Did Paul Really Say?

Women Deacons:

Paul could not specifically call women "deaconesses," because there was no Greek word meaning "servant" that was feminine. Just as *adam*, mankind, and so forth, the words *diakoneo* or *diakonos*[4] refer to both men and women. How do we know Paul meant both men and women? Look at First Timothy 3:8-13.

The entire chapter gives moral characteristics that church leaders should have. Verse 8 says that *deacons* should be worthy of respect and lists what their reputations should be. Then notice verse 11. It is very important.

> **[The] women likewise must be worthy of respect and serious, not gossipers, but temperate and self-controlled, [thoroughly] trustworthy in all things.**

This verse about women is right in the *middle* of his instructions about deacons. If he were not talking about women deacons, he would not talk of deacons just before and just after, nor would it be in the chapter or section with instructions for church leaders. Paul already made comments about how Christian women should act in the previous chapter.

Dr. J. Rodman Williams, professor of theology at Regent University, Virginia Beach, Virginia, puts it this way:

This statement (about the women) is both preceded by (vv. 8-10) and followed by (vv. 12-13) specific words about deacons. Thus, it seems apparent that "the women" are also deacons, or deaconesses. . . . The diaconate therefore may include both men and women. The first qualification listed for deacons — that they "be serious" (1 Timothy 3:8) — is likewise stated for the women (v. 11). . . .[5]

The word *women* in verse 11 is the Greek *gynaikas*, a form of *gyne*.[6] It *can* also be translated "wife." The context determines whether it is women or wives being talked about.

The *King James Version* of the Bible, *The New International Version* of the Bible, and *The New English Bible* add the word "Their" in front of this word — when it is not there in the original Greek — in order to translate verse 11 as "Their wives" instead of [The] women, as in *The Amplified Version*. However, at least *The Amplified* shows you the article. [The] has been added and is not in the original.[7]

Williams comments, "Why should Paul single out the wives of deacons rather than [the wives of] overseers (elders) for particular discussion?"[8]

Bishops' wives should have a stricter lifestyle even. Yet he does not mention "wives" of any other church offices. So why would he single out "deacons' wives"? Were they more apt to be unruly or out of order? I do not think so! It seems totally illogical that Paul meant anything but "women deacons."

Williams believes the Early Church deaconesses only assisted with ministries to women. However, he does say an order of deaconesses was established that was viewed more as assistants to the clergy than as women deacons that "went into eclipse for many centuries, but has been revived in a number of Protestant churches."[9]

Paul's admonitions about women in the previous chapter (1 Timothy 2:11,12) are paraphrased from the original in this way by one author:

Women should not distract from the service by inquiries, but should instead prepare to inquire at home of their own husbands. For I do not permit a woman to teach a man in any way *as to usurp authority* over him, for Adam was formed first and then Eve. Therefore, after she has received an education in the Word of God, she is permitted to speak and participate, the same as the men.[10]

Paul's instructions to Timothy continue his "model" order for church services and are not specifically dealing with women apart from how to act in a service. Also, remember that he was still writing to churches primarily made up of Greeks, whose women had a lot of liberty in public.

As for Paul's references to women preachers, pastors, prophets, or even apostles, most Christians do not know they are in the Bible because male translators have presented the passages in light of traditional gender bias.

In other words, they have not believed women could possibly be used in ministry, so they adjust the interpretations to fit that belief.

It always pays to study the original Hebrew or Greek and the history of the Church and the times in which the Bible was written.

What About Women in a Fivefold Office?

One particular woman whom most believe pastored with her husband, Aquila, was named Priscilla. (Acts 18:2.) In Acts 18:18, Priscilla is mentioned first, as also in Acts 18:26, where she is mentioned first as teaching an early convert, Apollos. In Romans 16:3, Paul wrote, **Give my greetings to Prisca and Aquila, my fellow workers in Christ Jesus**.

They are included as "fellow workers" with her name first. The first time the couple is mentioned, the husband's name is first — which would have been the usual manner of address for a couple.

Then in First Corinthians 16:19, the fact that this couple had a church in their home is mentioned.

Other women, such as Tryphena, Tryphosa, and Persis in Romans 16:12, could all have been pastors, from the way Paul's greeting is worded. However, this cannot be determined beyond the shadow of a doubt.

It *is* clear beyond the shadow of a doubt that women were mentioned along with men as "fellow workers" — which would be contradictory if Paul's comments about women being silent in church was a general instruction, not something for a particular situation.

Women Prophets:

One very clear passage about women in ministry involves the evangelist Philip's four daughters, who are clearly called "prophetesses" in Acts 21:9. The Greek word is *propheteuo*, which comes from *prophetes*, the word translated "prophet" in the list of five-fold offices.[11] (Ephesians 4:11.) Were they also to be "silent" in church services?

Women Apostles:

One woman mentioned in Paul's writings was included by him among the apostles!

> **Salute Andronicus and Junia, my kinsmen** (my relations), **and my fellowprisoners, who are of note among the apostles, who also were in Christ before me.**
>
> **Romans 16:7 KJV**

You see, *Junia* is the feminine form of a Latin male name, "Junius." This relation of Paul's, who was converted even before he was, apparently also was considered an apostle. In this case, gender bias led the *Amplified Bible* translators to think an apostle could not possibly be a woman, so they added an "s" to Junia to make it male!

However, in the original Greek, the word definitely is *Junia*, a female. Also, "Junias" would be incorrect if Paul was referring to a man. The Latin male name is *Junius*.

To sum up, then, Paul's concern with women being silent, and so forth, involved situations where they were out of order or usurping authority, which is a sin for man *or* woman.

Other comments concerned their modesty in public — again, aimed at Greek women, because Jewish women's clothes already covered them, sometimes even to a veil such as Arab women wear today.

Some of his other instructions concerned proper attitudes in marriage. Therefore, when these three situations are confused — and when specific comments for specific situations are taken out of context and applied as general principles across the board for all women at all times and places — we have gotten wrong interpretations of Scripture.

Too many men, as well as some women, have used the traditional gender-bias interpretations of Paul's writings to keep women "in their place." The truth is that, since Jesus came, He has been trying to *restore* women to their rightful place!

The Bible teaches that we are all, male and female, part of a royal priesthood. (1 Peter 2:9.)

[1]Jeremias, Joachim. *Jerusalem in the Time of Jesus*, (Philadelphia, PA: Fortress Press, 1969), pp. 359-373.
[2]Trombley, pp. 135,136.
[3]Pickett.
[4]Strong's, "Greek Dictionary," p. 22, #'s 1247, 1249.
[5]Rodman, J. William. *Renewal Theology*, Vol. 3, "The Church, the Kingdom, and Last Things," (Grand Rapids, MI: Zondervan Publishing House, 1992), p. 210.
[6]Ibid, Footnote #247.
[7]Ibid.
[8]Ibid.
[9]Ibid, Footnote 251.
[10]Vinnett, *For Women Only*, pp. 98,99.
[11]Strong's, p. 62, #'s 4395, 4396.

6

A Royal Priesthood

But you are a chosen race, a royal priesthood, a dedicated nation, [God's] own purchased, special people, that you may set forth the wonderful deeds ... of Him Who called you out of darkness into His marvelous light.

1 Peter 2:9

God said the husband is the head of the wife. Yet, we have called him the priest of the home. The Bible does not say that. Again, that is mixing authority in marriage with authority in the Church, or in the Kingdom, or in Christ.

To say that husbands are the heads of their homes but not the priests of their homes is not a matter of semantics. It is a matter of assignment, of delegated authority, as opposed to rank in the Kingdom of God. In my meetings, I tell the men they do not want me to preach about their delegated authority in marriage, because being the head of the home involves much more than being a priest!

The Bible teaches us, saints, that we are all part of a royal priesthood. We are all called to be priests, male and female together. That wonderful realm of authority that God delegated is marvelous. But we must not give the male authority that God did *not* give him, nor must we take away the authority that God *did* give him.

The majority of Christians think God named Eve; however, the Bible says that Adam named her, just as he had all the other creations of God.

> **Then Adam said . . . She shall be called Woman, because she was taken out of a man** (Genesis 2:23). **The man called his wife's name Eve (life-spring), because she was the mother of all living** (Genesis 3:20).

Now look at Genesis 5:1 for the next step in the progression of mankind:

> **This is the book — the written record — of the generations of the off-spring of Adam. When God created man He made him in the likeness of God.**

When God created man, it was in His own likeness. However, after the fall, notice that man is now in the likeness of Adam. *After the fall*, Adam named his wife Eve. God did not name her — He already had named *them* as *adam*. Here we begin to see the generations of Adam, not Jesus. The male *adam* begot sons in his own image. We were born with the nature of Adam.

The carnal nature comes from our father Adam, not from our Father God. God knew we had no way of changing back into His image by ourselves, so He designed the costly plan of redemption through the blood of His own Son, Jesus.

Two-thirds of the Church world today is trying to act like Jesus. We do not have that ability in our Adamic natures. Jesus was the express image of the Father, sent to live in us by the power of the Holy Spirit. Until the image to which we have been restored in our innermost nature takes over our minds and emotions, we cannot be like Jesus.

You cannot try to be like Jesus without the Holy Spirit. For years people have tried, especially denominations that reject the infilling of the Holy Spirit. Our souls (minds, wills, and emotions) need to be permeated with the Holy Spirit. When we are born again as new creatures, He begins to change us from glory to glory. Then He fills our being like He wanted to do before man ever fell.

We are going to go home to Heaven in His image, complete and mature, but not without the Holy Spirit. The more I am willing to give up my self-image, the more of God's image I can receive. Good-bye, Adam. Today, I am not going to have your image. You are dead, your nature is dead in me, and dead people do not talk.

Today, the image of God is going to be allowed to operate in my life. Being changed from glory to glory is not the same as being challenged. Being challenged will not take you home in His image. Only being changed will do that.

By the action of Calvary, we are being changed into Christ's image so male and female can walk together as one, each with his and her own delegated authority.

God has put both into Christ, not as male or female, but as mankind walking with Him. Husbands and wives, male preachers, female preachers, male leaders, female leaders — doing what? We are to walk "in the cool of the day" with Jesus talking to us, fellowshipping with us, giving us authority, changing us into His image.

Christians Need To Accept Restoration

In the last Adam, God is restoring what we would have had if our first parents had not fallen. It is glorious indeed to see God restoring men and women together as one, seeing them fulfill their delegated responsibilities and yet allowing both to be the servants of God He has called them to be.

As God delivers His Church from the bondage of tradition and culture and from fallen man's doctrine of divine order, we will see men and women functioning together to build godly homes and fulfill God's purpose in the building of His Church. However, it must start in the home.

As redemption cleanses us from the desire of men to rule over women, and women in today's world to rule over men, men and women will not be threatened by each other. Instead, we will welcome the godly counsel of one another. How can one-half of the being made in the image of God not have godly counsel simply because that half is female?

God pours out His Spirit on His sons and His daughters alike. We are in Christ, the Second, and Last, Man, who did not fail or fall, and in Him everything is being restored to fulfill God's plan.

It is very important to notice Genesis 5:2, just after we are told that the male *adam* named the female "Eve." The very next statement reiterates, confirms, reinforces what God did with Adam and Eve.

He created them male and female and blessed them, and named them [both] Adam at the time when they were created.

Genesis 5:2

Here, God made a point of reaffirming that male and female were one, and both *adam*, equal in being named stewards to have dominion over His created beings.

The more we are willing to give up our image the more of God's image we can receive. The key thing here is that it is time for male *adams* to realize there are two genders in this royal priesthood, and neither should be usurping the other's delegated authority.

We should be able to submit to one another according to the giftedness. God is saying it is time for the Body of Christ to become one. The only way it is going to become that way is for us to stop fighting, obey the Word of God, and begin to submit to one another.

We must get ourselves together and function according to the delegated authority and giftings of God.

Women must be free in the natural as they already are declared legally free in the spirit realm.

7

Women: Be Free

Christ purchased our freedom (redeeming us) from the curse (doom) of the Law's (condemnation), by [Himself] becoming a curse for us, for it is written [in the Scriptures], Cursed is everyone who hangs on a tree (is crucified).

Galatians 3:13

A longer and more specific title for this chapter would be, "Women, Be Free To Take Your God-Given Places in the Body of Christ."

Christ purchased our freedom, redeeming us from the curse of the Law. That includes the cultural laws and by the time of Jesus in Judah, women were considered property. Some of that cultural flavoring was carried over into the New Testament church. The apostles had to deal with the merging of "Jew and Gentile" and the tearing down of the wall of hostility in the natural.

If we do not read their writings in light of the cultural context, the mixing of cultures in the early Church, some of the scriptures will look as if women were still in bondage. If we match every comment about women with the bottom-line truth that, in Christ, there is no difference of gender, it will be easier to understand what was being said.

If what any New Testament writer says about women contradicts what Jesus said, then the right thing to do is look for what the passage really means. The wrong thing is to throw out one of the passages because we believe the other.

Even more wrong is to match the passages against "traditions of men," which Jesus told the Pharisees made God's Word null and void, or "of no effect." (Mark 7:8-13.) That is exactly what has been done, first with women and then with race. Did you know the "woman question" has been around a lot longer than the race question?

God said that it is time for us to be free, and in order for the entire body to get free, in order for the body to mature, in order for the body to be completely whole, everyone has to be fitted in place.

> **[Come] and as living stones be yourselves built [into] a spiritual house, for a holy (dedicated, consecrated) priesthood, to offer up [those] spiritual sacrifices [that are] acceptable and well-pleasing to God through Jesus Christ.**
>
> **1 Peter 2:5**

You cannot exclude a part of the body, then expect the body to become healthy, mature, and whole. It is not going to happen if the present situation continues.

Jesus did the redeeming. He set women free from the status they had held since the fall. It is two millennia past time for us to believe it and begin to occupy the place God has set for us. Jesus Christ purchased our freedom and redeemed us from all that was under the curse.

Sometimes we only consider that He redeemed us from sin, He redeemed us from sickness, He redeemed us from poverty — and that is all true. However, the curse took in a lot more. The curse meant that some people were more equal than others!

There was a difference under the Law according to who you were and who your parents were. It made a difference whether or not you were free or slave, Jew or Gentile, or male or female. However, Jesus purchased every single person who accepted Him. If we do not take what He has given us, we are going to make His sacrifice of none effect.

Look at Galatians 3:26: **For in Christ Jesus you are all sons of God through faith.** Years ago when I read that, I thought he was only talking to men. I did not then understand that when God says "sons" He is not referring to gender. He was talking to a Body of people who had accepted Jesus and were in Christ.

Paul wrote that we are *all* sons of God through faith, all were baptized into Christ, into a spiritual union and communion with Christ. That means being born again of the Spirit of Christ. After defining who the "sons of God" are, Paul went on to say there is no distinction any longer based on earthly divisions among people.

Where before, under the curse of being in the Adamic nature and under the Old Covenant Law, there was a distinction. Now there is no more distinction to God.

If a non-Jewish person accepted Jesus, they are as much a son of God as a Jew who accepted Jesus.

If a slave accepted Jesus Christ, they are as much a son of God as a free man who accepted Jesus.

If a woman accepted Jesus, she is as much a son of God as a man who accepted Jesus.

That verse was not just for the early Christians. Change the past tense to present and future — "accepts or will accept" Jesus — and it is still eternally true.

Christ the Anointed One has purchased all of mankind and freed us from the entire curse of the Law. We are sinning if we continue to let anyone hinder us from operating in the freedom spelled out for us in Galatians.

Authority Is Neither Male Nor Female

Authority has no gender, even in the natural world. It is neither masculine nor feminine. It is the right to operate in a certain office because you have been legally elected or appointed to that office — or because you are the husband, the father or mother, the boss, the principal of a school, and so forth.

Because of our social traditions and because of the confusion in the interpretation of the Word of God, women have cowered back too long from fulfilling our callings. We have allowed the enemy to tell us that anytime we gain maturity, or manifest any kind of zeal, or walk in any kind of authority, that we have a Jezebel spirit.

We need to understand that a person with a "Jezebel spirit" can be a male or a female. That is a person who is usurping authority over someone with rightful authority. The term comes from Queen Jezebel, wife of King Ahab of Israel (the northern ten and a half tribes), in Elijah's day.

She ran the nation from behind the throne. Ahab was "henpecked," we might say in today's colloquialisms. He was "wimpy" and did not fulfill his role as head of the house and king of the country. She was a high priestess of Baal and usurped his authority.

That has nothing to do with spiritual zeal, excitement, or commitment. Answering a call of God on your life is not rebellion against men, but obedience to God. It is not operating under "a Jezebelic spirit" to do what God has assigned you to do.

God always refers to a believer in the male gender. It is important that we realize that and understand why He does that. God says it is time for His women to be set free so that the Body can become healthy.

God has called every one of His sons to have that spiritual zeal and commitment and excitement.

There are two Greek words translated "son" in the New Testament. The one most used is *huios*;[1] the other is *teknon*.[2]

"Sons" as applied to Christians means both males and females who have been reborn in the image of God. It means those who show maturity and likeness to God's character irrespective of gender. This definition ties right in with the scriptures in Galatians 3:28.

All who have put on Christ, the Anointed One, have been baptized into Christ meaning they are clothed with the righteousness of Jesus the Messiah. When God sees us, He sees His son clothed in the anointing. He never sees gender.

What God sees is a vessel clothed in the anointing of Jesus, because it is the *anointing* that carries out the ministry. It is not the gender that does the ministry.

So many have missed it in the Body of Christ by confusing gender with calling and anointing of the Holy Spirit.

I believe we are going to see God's original plan begin to come to fruition in our lifetimes. How God begins something is how He finishes it. Even if it gets off course, God always has a way to keep His plan on track.

In Galatians, Paul was saying we are now restored to where God began in Genesis. First John 3:9 uses the masculine pronouns, yet he is referring to males or females:

> **No one born (begotten) of God [deliberately and knowingly] habitually practices sin, for God's nature abides in him — His principle of life, the divine sperm, remains permanently within him — and he cannot practice sinning because he is born (begotten) of God.**

God said, "It is time for women to be free to be all I created them to be."

I am never going into bondage again, and I was in bondage for so long. Now we do not have to get into rebellion in order to be free, we just have to walk in what God created us to be.

It upsets me every time I walk through the mall and see women from other nations covered up, even their faces, with their eyebrows the only parts of them showing. Then the man they are with has on American clothes, American watches, and American haircuts, while she looks like some kind of slave.

I want to say, "Woman, you are free in Jesus."

In 90-degree temperatures, you cannot tell me she is not miserable. Sad to say, some Western women do not have sheets over their faces, but in reality, they are as bound as those Eastern and African women.

When Did Women Receive Power?

In the restoration of man into the Second Race, the children of God and Abraham through Jesus received power to do His works on the Day of Pentecost — both men and women. Jesus prophesied it, then some days later, it happened.

> **But you shall receive power — ability, efficiency and might — when the Holy Spirit has come upon you; and you shall be My witnesses in Jerusalem and all Judea and Samaria and to the ends — the very bounds — of the earth.**
>
> **Acts 1:8**

Jesus prophesied that the outpouring of the Holy Spirit was coming to make all recipients of Him witnesses to Jesus. He said everyone who received this power when the Holy Spirit came upon them would be witnesses of the Anointed One and His anointing.

I used to have a very limited understanding of what it meant to be a witness for Jesus. I thought it only meant telling people about Jesus. However, being "witnesses" has a much greater scope.

Being witnesses means we will do what He does and operate in the same anointing He did. We will be "imitations" of Him.

Being witnesses means when people see us they ought to see Jesus.

Being witnesses means we now have His nature; therefore, we can show Him to the world.

Jesus said the Spirit of God was coming to make all the members of His Body witnesses that, as the Son of God, He truly exists, that He was born a man, lived, died, and was resurrected. His Body includes all who will receive His power, ability, efficiency, and might.

Jesus was saying, "As My representatives on earth, they will have the power to present Me to the rest of the Adamic race."

Let's see what really happened at Pentecost.

Did both men and women receive the Holy Spirit, or did the "tongues of fire" only rest on men?

[1]Strong's, "Greek Dictionary," p. 93, #5207.
[2]Ibid, p. 89, #5043.

8

What Happened at Pentecost?

And when they had entered [the city], they mounted to the upper room where they were indefinitely staying —— Peter and John and James and Andrew, Philip and Thomas, Bartholomew and Matthew, James the son of Alphaeus and Simon the Zealot and Judas the [son] of James.

Acts 1:13

The disciples were in "an upper room" for days **steadfastly in prayer** until the Day of Pentecost. (v. 14.) An "upper room" usually was a room built on top of a house, or sometimes separate from the house on a higher level.

Most houses had flat roofs in Jerusalem at that time. This room could have been the size of the whole house and like a sun room today, serving as a cooler place for people to sit or even sleep during hot weather. It also could be a guest room and smaller than the size of the house. The Shunammite woman built one for Elisha and called it "the prophet's room." (2 Kings 4:10.)

So they were *all* in this upper room waiting for the Holy Spirit. *Now it was not just men in that upper room.* How do I know? I know the same way you can — from reading the very next verse:

All of these with their minds in full agreement devoted themselves steadfastly to prayer, [waiting together] with *the women and Mary the mother of Jesus,* and with His brothers.

Acts 1:14

69

So you see that women as well as men were together waiting. What happened when the time of waiting ended? Did the Holy Spirit descend only on the men? Look at Acts 2:1-4:

> **And when the day of Pentecost had fully come, they were all assembled together in one place** (the Upper Room), **when suddenly there came a sound from heaven like the rushing of a violent tempest blast, and it filled the whole house in which they were sitting. And there appeared to them tongues resembling fire, which were separated and distributed and which settled on each one of them. And they were all filled — diffused throughout their souls — with the Holy Spirit and began to speak with other (different, foreign) languages, as the Spirit kept giving them clear and loud expression (in each tongue in appropriate words).**

Who were assembled together? *All of them, men and women.*

Who saw the tongues that looked like fire? *All of them did.*

Who were the ones on whom the tongues settled? *All of them.*

Who were filled with the Holy Spirit? *All of them.*

Who began to speak with other languages? *All of them.*

Luke wrote that *all* who were assembled received the same experience, both the men and the women alike.

They *all* were diffused throughout with the same power to do what? All were filled with the power to be witnesses, to be His representatives. Jesus did not leave women out. If He had not included them on the Day of Pentecost, then perhaps people could make a real case that women were not called to be His witnesses.

However, God made sure women were included, and Jesus even had His mother there. What happened next? The group was heard by the crowds outside who had come from all over the known world for the Feast of Pentecost. Those people thought the group bursting out of the upper room were drunk.

> **But Peter, standing with the eleven, raised his voice and addressed them: You Jews and all you residents of**

Jerusalem, let this be [explained] to you so that you will know and understand; listen closely to what I have to say. For these men are not drunk, as you imagine. . . .

Acts 2:14,15

If you all look at that phrase, **for these men**, and do not look at the previous verses that say *all* of those there were filled and understand that everyone, or all, included the women in Acts 1:13,14, you might think only men were involved.

However, the Bible does not contradict itself. So rather than throw out the verses about women being included as error because the "men only" fits traditional thinking, let us look at this situation and see what happened. When we do, we can see that the verses do not contradict themselves.

Spiritual Change Affects Society

Both men and women waited, both men and women had the Holy Spirit descend as tongues of fire on them, both men and women were infilled with the Holy Spirit.

However, then we get from what happened in God to how the group had to present themselves in a cultural setting of the time. If the women had come out front and started to preach, as Peter did, the crowd probably would have stoned all of them. That would have been the same in the Jewish culture as the situation with the woman taken in adultery. (John 8:3.)

The very idea that women were displaying themselves in public and daring to talk to men! That would have offended every man in the crowd and incited them to the heights of religious mania. Even in today's climate in some of the Arabic countries where women are covered top to toe and counted as property — what would happen if one of those women just lowered her veil and began to make a speech in the public square?

I promise you she would be torn limb from limb, stoned, or killed in some other way without a trial or without a hearing of any kind.

This crowd on the Day of Pentecost was not like the Corinthians, Ephesians, or Galatians and the other Greek and Roman cultures to which Paul ministered. This was a totally Jewish group where women had an entirely different place.

In the Greek/Roman towns and cities, Paul had to tell women to "cool it," to stop running over those in authority in the Church.

In the Jewish communities, there was no outward move that we can see to ease women into more public roles. Why not, if Jesus had restored equality of dominion? That is because such a move would have pulled the emphasis off Jesus and onto women and would really have stirred up persecution against the early Christians.

Persecution for the Word's sake was something that had to be endured. However, persecution for social revolution was not something Jesus advocated or instigated. The point is that Jesus always changed society from the inside out, not through causes and social issues.

Being a witness for Him means bringing the truth about Him to more and more people, some of whom at least will receive Him. The ones who receive Him — if they truly walk in the light — will change society because they are changed.

Peter went on to proclaim that times had changed, Old Testament had given way to New, and old prophecies were now being fulfilled. The prophecy he was inspired by the Holy Spirit to declare was being fulfilled that day *involved both men and women*.

If that crowd had truly listened — and obviously some of them did — they would have seen that women were being restored. What Peter quoted were God's words through the Prophet Joel of the time when His Spirit would be poured out on all His children, both men and women.

Peter was saying, "What you just saw take place in this upper room with these *men and women* is the fulfillment of what Joel promised us from God."

If we look at the events of chapters just following this, you can see women begin to be given a more equal place in church life. When Ananias lied to the Holy Spirit and dropped dead, his wife Sapphira not long after appeared before the disciples, told the same lie (spoke in public meeting), and also dropped dead.

In Ephesians 1:22,23, Paul tells us more about Jesus as Head and what that means to us.

And He has put all things under His feet and has appointed Him the universal and supreme Head of the church (a headship exercised throughout the church).

Verse 22

So God has put all things under the Lord's feet and has appointed the Lord the universal and supreme Head of the Church, a headship exercised throughout the Church which is His Body.

Which is His body, the fullness of Him who fills all in all — for in that body lives the full measure of Him Who makes everything complete, and Who fills everything everywhere [with Himself].

Verse 23

What was Paul telling us? Christ Jesus has been appointed the Head of the Church. The Church is His Body. His Body — us, male and female Christians — has received a full measure of Him and everything is complete in Him. The entire Church, both male and female, are always referred as His Body.

Never again after this time will you see men and women referred to by gender when things of the Spirit are being discussed. The only time you will see God refer to male and female is when it has to do with the natural marital relationship.

Whenever you see the Body of Jesus spoken of, it is always referred to in the male gender, "he or him." The reason is because Galatians 3:26 and 28 have told us we are all the sons of God and no more male or female. We are all one in Him.

All Were Given the Life of Christ

God gave us — male and female — the very life of Christ Himself even when we were "dead" through our own shortcomings and trespasses. Paul writing to the Christians at Ephesus, spelled out in detail what God did for all mankind and how rich, great, wonderful, and intense His love is for us. (Ephesians 2:4.)

> **... He made us alive together in fellowship and in union with Christ — He gave us the very life of Christ Himself, the same new life with which He quickened Him. . . . And He raised us up together with Him and made us sit down together — giving us joint seating with Him — in the heavenly sphere [by virtue of our being] in Christ Jesus, the Messiah, the Anointed One.**
>
> **Ephesians 2:5,6**

He raised the entire body. Jesus did not leave one part down and one part up. He did not raise one part and leave another part out. He gave us joint seating with Jesus, both male and female. In actuality, that has not happened yet because all things have not been put under Jesus' feet in the natural. (Hebrews 2:8.) Yet it is already a spiritual reality.

That means we now have access to the throne of Jesus Christ where all of our needs will be met. When He was resurrected to be seated at the right hand of the Father, He became our Mediator in Heaven (1 Timothy 2:5), and we became His representatives on earth.

In essence, the entire Body of Christ has been seated with Him, male and female alike, because *we are all in Him.* Ephesians 2:7-10 contains the key, the reason why God did this:

> **He did this that He might clearly demonstrate through the ages to come the immeasurable (limitless, surpassing) riches of His free grace (His unmerited favor) in kindness and goodness of heart toward us in Christ Jesus. For it is by free grace (God's unmerited favor) that you are saved (delivered from judgment and made partakers of Christ's salvation) through [your] faith. And this [salvation] is not of your-**

selves — of your own doing, it came not through your own striving — but it is the gift of God; not because of works [not the fulfillment of the Law's demands], lest any man should boast. . . . For we are God's [own] handiwork (His workmanship), recreated in Christ Jesus. . . .

Here in this 10th verse, we are referred to the very beginning of mankind once again. God created *adam*, male and female, and now Paul writes that we *all* are God's handiwork and have been *recreated* in Jesus.

Why were we recreated in Jesus? The rest of the 10th verse tells us our purpose after being restored, which is to do what He "predestined" (arranged from the beginning of the world) for us to do.

In Jesus, God finished or completed what He had ordained for mankind. God had a prepared plan for His children to walk the good life — not secondary life, not second-hand citizen life — but the *good life*. Adam and Eve forfeited that, but Jesus restored the right to a good life to us.

Jesus has designated all those born again since His resurrection as His Body. However, the Body has many members, just like a human body. So who places the members in the Body? God does, just as He arranged the parts of the human body. We belong to Him, having been bought with a price (the life of Jesus on the cross). (1 Corinthians 6:20.)

He is the potter, and we are the clay. (Isaiah 45:9, 64:8; Romans 9:21.) How can one piece of clay say to another, "You are not equal with me. You cannot have as useful a place in the Body as I do"?

But as it is, God has placed and arranged the limbs and organs in the body, each (particular one) of them, just as He wished and saw fit and with the best adaptation. But if [the whole] were all a single organ, where would the body be?

1 Corinthians 12:18,19

If the whole Body were all men, what would the Body be?

If the whole Body were all women, what would the Body be?

If the whole Body were all Jews, what would the Body be?

If the whole Body were all non-Jews, what would it be?

If the whole Body were free men or slaves, what would be the result?

In any of those cases, the Body would be unbalanced, incomplete, not a restored oneness.

> **And now there are [certainly] many limbs and organs, but a single body. And the eye is not able to say to the hand, I have no need of you, nor again the head to the feet, I have no need of you.**
>
> **1 Corinthians 12:20,21**

Neither can the male *adam* say to the female *adam*, I do not need you.

> **But instead, there is [absolute] necessity for the parts of the body that are considered the more weak.**
>
> **1 Corinthians 12:22**

God is beginning to honor "the weaker vessels" as well as the stronger. You hear about very few women who fall once they get in leadership positions. They have been kept under for so long that when God does use them, they are really committed.

God is telling us something different now. It has appeared that women are less important, but watch God now and see what He does. Get in your places, ladies, and God can use you. So that there shall be no division, God is going to do it.

So there will be **no division or discord or lack of adaptation (of the parts of the body to each other)**, God is bringing us to the place where all of the members of the Body **have a mutual interest in and care for one another**. (1 Corinthians 12:25).

God is bringing us together whether we all like it or not. He is bringing us to the place where, if one suffers, all the other members suffer. (1 Corinthians 12:26.) As long as there continues to be division and rejection of one part of the body for another, racial or gender-wise, everyone is going to suffer.

The Body cannot come to wholeness and be healthy until the division stops.

If one member suffers, all the parts share the suffering.

If one member is honored, all members share in the enjoyment of it.

Therefore, anyone who thinks they can make it without women being given a place alongside men will never move to a place of total honor in God. The enemy's greatest desire is to keep the entire Body of Christ from the oneness that Jesus prayed about in John 17.

We are all God's "sons," and it is time now for women to take the rightful places that God has given us. *Cast down the intimidation* and go forward in the Anointed Christ.

9

Cast Down Intimidation!

For [the Spirit which] you have now received [is] not a spirit of slavery to put you once more in bondage to fear, but you have received the Spirit of adoption — the Spirit producing sonship — in [the bliss of] which we cry, Abba! [That is,] Father!

Romans 8:15

Women, when you operate in ministry, you are not operating as a female — and neither does a man in ministry operate as a male. Both minister as "sons" who work for and represent Jesus in the earth.

Therefore, women need to cast off any intimidation and come out of fear. You have received the spirit of adoption just as the men in the Body, and the Holy Spirit testifies (or witnesses) with your own spirit that you are called and anointed.

It is time we let the Holy Spirit testify with our spirits to assure us that we are *equal* children of God.

For (even the whole) creation (all nature) waits expectantly and longs earnestly for God's sons to be made known — waits for the revealing, the disclosing of their sonship.

Romans 8:19

Stop limiting yourself, ladies! The Bible says Jesus' Body has all of His fullness, and everyone in His Body is able to walk in completeness in everything. That is because He has filled everyone everywhere who has received Him with Himself, with His anointing, with the essence, the nature, and the character of God.

Christ Jesus has been appointed the Head of the Church, His Body has received a full measure of Himself, and everything is complete in Him.

All you need is a revelation.

All you need is to see the blueprint God has shown us in His Word.

All you need is to get rid of all that garbage that has "programmed" your brain into believing that women cannot minister.

For years, I could only see myself as an evangelist, because that is what everyone called me from the time I was ordained.

Finally, I said, "First of all, God, You have never told me I was an evangelist. I am not an evangelist. That is not the only thing a woman can be when she is called to preach."

Many women have not come forth into their full ministries because they have called themselves evangelists and allowed others to call them "an evangelist." Perhaps some are evangelists, but what about those called to other offices?

You will never be truly an evangelist if that is not what God called you to be, and you are hindering yourself from being what He did call you to be. Cast off intimidation from denominations, male ministers, and anyone else trying to fit you into a preconceived image. Let God identify who you are.

Somehow, in some churches, women could be accepted as evangelists, who call people to salvation but do not teach men, but not in other offices. Therefore, even when women were known to be called, they had to be evangelists.

Some of you are pastors. Some of you are prophets, but you cannot ever fulfill that call if you keep calling yourself an evangelist. If you are an evangelist, you will be anointed and have a peaceful spirit about that calling. You will have the grace to walk in that office, but do not call yourself something you are not.

Some of you have called yourself evangelist so long that you have cursed your calling in the spirit realm. You need to seek God as to your true calling, then repent and cancel those words that endorsed a wrong calling.

Some of you have been called as pastors or prophets, yet your people cannot hear your voice, because you have called yourself an evangelist. You must cancel those words when God did not say that.

He is not obligated to anoint you to do anything but what He created you to be from before the foundation of the world. (Ephesians 2:10.)

He will not anoint you if you have called yourself to some other office than the one He designated for you.

When all of this began to come together for me, I told the devil, "I got free today. I became your worst nightmare. I intend to reclaim every year you stole from me. I wake up every morning, decreeing and declaring who I am. I have canceled those words spoken against me and those words labeling me something I am not."

First, Find Your True Calling

This is the reason some women in the ministry are struggling so. They are plagued with words spoken over them that are not accurate. They are not sure of what place they really have or what they really are called to do.

Women, you need to remember that you have been set free by Jesus, and whom the Son sets free ought to stay free.

> **. . . If you abide in My Word — hold fast to My teachings and live in accordance with them — you are truly My disciples. And you will know the truth, and *the truth will set you free.***

> **John 8:31,32**

That could not be plainer:

*Abide in His Word, study it for the truth.

*Hold fast to the teachings of Jesus.

*Live according to those teachings.

*That way, you will know what is God's truth.

*That truth will set you free.

What are we set free from? Not just sin and eternal separation from God (the second death — Revelation 20:14), but from prejudice, limitations of man, poverty, sickness and disease, and all of the ills of the fallen world.

You have inherited all things through a covenant (an eternal contract) that will ensure you there will be nothing missing, nothing broken, and nothing lacking in your life. (Hebrews 8:7-22.)

> **But now in Christ Jesus, you who once were [so] far away, through (by, in) the blood of Christ have been brought near. For He is [Himself] our peace — our bond of unity and harmony. He has made us both [Jew and Gentile] one (body), and has broken down (destroyed, abolished) the hostile dividing wall between us.**
>
> **Ephesians 2:13,14**

The Christ in you, not Jesus seated in Heaven who has orchestrated everything, but the Holy Spirit in you will see to it that you walk in that bond of unity and harmony *as long as you allow Him to.*

What do you think? God was just going to break down the wall between Jew and Gentile and not break down the wall between male and female, when He said there is neither male nor female.

So if Jesus' blood has broken down, destroyed, and abolished the hostile dividing wall between us, there cannot be any more walls. However, we act in unreality, not spiritual reality. Therefore, traditional attitudes keep the Church living *as if the walls were still there*!

The only reason the barrier is still in society between races, classes, and genders is because we are artificially keeping the walls up. The only reason women are limited in ministry is because many Christians have been listening to lies from the enemy and the opinions of humans.

It is not just men keeping the walls up. Other women are some of the worst critics of female ministers. The reason a lot of women will put down women in ministry is because they are so bound that they are angry others have even a little bit of freedom.

I have tasted freedom, and I know the truth from the Book. The only reason I can be hindered from anything I need to do would be a lack of prayer and not preparing the atmosphere to release my ministry. I am a tither and a giver. My eyes are open. I can see what I am supposed to do. I have vision and can see purpose. Nothing can hinder me.

God considers all of us in Christ — His Body of witnesses with no superiority of gender. We are commanded to walk after the Spirit, not after our lower nature which is flesh. God chose each believer's place in His Son's body with no distinctions.

The male parts of the Body cannot legitimately say to the female parts of the Body, "We don't want you. God can't use you. You are not really a part of the Body of Christ because you are a woman!"

There Should Be No Competition

Collectively, we are the Anointed One's Body. God wants His female expression as much as He does His male expression. Each must be set in a God-appointed place in order to function in unity and oneness.

We refer to one another as male and female because that is the way it is in the natural. However, when it comes to spiritual things, we are all His sons, heirs of his inheritance. The enemy's greatest desire is to keep the entire Body of Christ from the oneness that Jesus prayed for in John 17.

The Body cannot come to complete wholeness and maturity without all of God's sons being revealed in their proper places of function, uninhibited by error, division, and traditions of men.

We need to get delivered from competitiveness and jealousy, not just men versus women, but women who compete with one another. The Bible says that from before the foundation of the world, God chose who I would be and what I would do. (Ephesians 1:4.) Is that not right? Just as He chose what you would be and what you would do.

When I recognize the awesomeness of God's mind to design me individually, why would I be jealous of someone else when God made me to be all that He made me to be, and I like myself. So find out who you are supposed to be. Start liking yourself, then you will help celebrate with me.

Then we will not be stopping up the spirit realm with all that negative mess. Every time you speak something negative against someone else, you hinder that person, for we are all connected, whether we believe it or not.

All of our ministries cannot be exactly the same, because God did not order them to be alike. God chose the levels. Some ministries will go higher than others. It does not mean either is better than the other. It simply means that is where God placed them.

I would like to sing like some of the sisters I hear in my meetings.

I would like to preach like some of the well-known women ministers.

I would like to prophesy like some of my feminine counterparts.

However, I am not jealous of any of them who are better than me at anything God sets us to do. Why do I feel that way? It is because we need one another. I need to be in unity with them, and they need to be in unity with me.

Men and women need to study the Word about women in ministry as I have, not just accept traditional thinking. Any wisdom and understanding about "the woman question" are in the Word of God.

I would rather study the Bible than eat natural food, and I really mean that. Perhaps you have not been as tormented or bound or tested or tried as I was. The person I am now is not the person I was several years ago.

If I wrote half of where I came from, you would not believe that I am the same militant woman who stands before crowds of people declaring who I am in Christ. I was tormented by what man thinks and very intimidated.

God told me one morning, "It is your own fault. Get in the Bible and reprogram your mind."

Once I did that, I was set free. Praise the Lord, today I am not intimidated by anybody.

God gave each one in His Body His glory and His honor. You have it, and I have it, so that we will be equally one in Him. Each one of us has inherited in our inner man the nature of God. That is Christ in us, our hope of glory. He calls us all His "sons."

So, *cast down intimidation*, all of you female *adams* called by God to fulfill His plan and do His work, and set about doing what you are called to do!

When you know you are free and equal in the Kingdom, the only reason you cannot have a worldwide ministry — if God has said that is what He plans for you — is because your mind is too small to believe it.

10

Is Your World Too Small?

For we are God's [own] handiwork (His workmanship), recreated in Christ Jesus, [born anew] that we may do those good works which God predestined (planned beforehand) for us, (taking paths which He prepared ahead of time) that we should walk in them — living the good life which He pre-arranged and made ready for us to live.

Ephesians 2:10

The only reason you cannot see who you are in Christ, what your place is in the Church, or what your calling is, is because your mind is too small, so to speak. Or it is because you are not looking at biblical truth and being distracted by natural thinking. God is here within us who are born again, and He wants Jesus' Body free!

What do I mean by your mind or world is too small? From the time we are born, our minds are being "programmed" like computers with ideas and concepts about ourselves and about the world in which we live. Whether you realize it or not, those ideas and concepts are *limitations*, or artificial walls, that determine how "big" you see the world.

Proverbs 23:7 says that, as a man thinks in his heart, that is the way he is. In other words, what and how you think has more effect on your life than almost anything else. That is why, when a person becomes born again, a recreated child of God adopted into His family as joint heir with Jesus, Paul wrote so many times that *your mind needs renewing*.

Unless you understand life yourself, and the world from the point of God's truth, at least part of what you think is deception. More and more in this century, the gap between the world's beliefs and biblical truth has widened and become obvious.

For example, there is evolution versus creationism . . . inevitable sickness and disease versus divine health and healing . . . focus on man as his own god and science as savior versus man is owned by God the Creator and Jesus as Savior, and so forth.

You can see that those views are totally incompatible, totally opposite and contrary to one another. Yet even many Christians try to believe both. That is being double-minded, trying to believe two opposite things at the same time. The result is that the world's view causes God's truths to be of no effect in that person's life.

How can you believe in divine healing if you also believe science is God?

How can you remain humble and have a servant's heart like Jesus if you think man is going to improve through science and get better and better?

The "walls" that determine the size and scope of your world are those things you believe.

How can you operate as a woman called of God to pastor or be an evangelist if you have "walls" in your mind that keep your world the size of your home and job and maybe the ministry of helps in the Church?

Obviously, you cannot! A double-minded person cannot receive of God because he or she is into doubt, not faith, and without faith, none of God's promises will work for you.

> **For truly, let not such a person imagine that he will receive anything [he asks for] from the Lord, [for being as he is] a man of two minds — hesitating, dubious, irresolute — [he is] unstable and unreliable and uncertain about everything (he thinks, feels, decides).**

> **James 1:7,8**

James also wrote that *if you lack wisdom*, ask of God who will give it to you liberally. (James 1:5.)

> **Only it must be in faith that he asks, with no wavering — no hesitating, no doubting. For the one who wavers (hesitates, doubts) is like the billowing surge out at sea, that is blown hither and thither and tossed by the wind.**

James 1:6

Are You Walking on God's Path?

I was told at one time that the only reason God was using me in ministry was because my husband was in rebellion and would not do what God wanted him to do. However, studying out the truth about God's intention for women *set me free*!

I found that my call, my purpose, my work, my ministry was set by God before I ever got here, before Pastor John Fortson ever existed in the earth. So I was not doing my husband's work. I was doing the work that God predestined for *me* to do.

Ephesians 2:10 in particular set me free. When my mind grasped the truth that God had predestined and planned a certain path for *me* — personally and individually and as a woman — even before creation, it expanded my world!

Before, I was like many women in ministry today. My world and ministry were bound by the "I can'ts." I cannot do this, and I cannot do that, because I was a woman, and women could not do certain things in the Church that men could.

Now, however, I can never get away with telling myself that I cannot do something, because every single thing that I am is already in me.

Everything I am called to do is already in me.

Everything that I will ever be is already in me.

Everything necessary for me to fulfill my life in Christ has been ordained and is within me.

Therefore, I did not have to believe the lie about what I could not do any longer. Once I saw truth, the "walls" in my mind fell, and I could begin to walk in those truths. The reason is that I had come to a conclusion a long time ago that whatever the Word said would be final authority in my life. No one can change my mind about that.

It took the fear of intimidation away from me to know that the Bible said there were paths already laid down by God for every day of my life. If you are born again, you also can be walking in a path God preordained for you.

The key word in that last sentence is *can*. If you "think" small or limited in your heart about God and His plan for you, you will not get very far on that path. If you believe man's traditions about women's roles and abilities, you will not walk a straight path but wander around in circles getting nowhere.

I once heard a pastor say he did not have a problem with God calling women into ministry. However, he doubted if women would ever have any large ministries or any real successful ministries. Did he think God has favorites?

At the very least, his world is so small that he thought women could preach — but not as good as men or not as powerfully or not as successfully. That also is being double-minded. That sounds as if God set me up to fail.

Why would He bother to call me to represent Him at all, if being female means I would not have a successful ministry?

My purpose and your purpose were ordained before the foundation of the world. It was in the mind of God, and He never released anything that was not good or that He did not intend to be successful.

Adam and Eve were "good" in God's eyes when created. It was not His plan or purpose for them to fail. Why did they fall, if He is omnipotent and all-knowing? That is because God's plan for man began with the concept that man would be a voluntary obedient and loving child.

In order to achieve that purpose, God had to allow man the right to choose. That means, of course, that man could choose wrongly. However, God foresaw that possibility and already had the plan made for Jesus to come as a man and die for the penalty of man's disobedience. Then those who received Jesus as the one who paid the price for them could be restored as children of God.

Satan was created the most beautiful being ever created and "perfect in his ways" (Ezekiel 28:15), yet he rebelled. However, there was and is no way back for him and his angels, because they apparently were never given the right to choose.

Angelic beings have the ability to choose, but no right. Angels are each one of a kind, created to do certain things for God. They are not a race nor were they created in God's image. They have no rights in God except to obey.

Mankind was created a race in the image of God with the right to choose. Of course, if you choose wrongly, and do not repent and accept the atonement made for your disobedience and rebellion, you will spend eternity with those beings who had no right to choose. (Revelation 20:14.)

For, as we all know, He [Christ] did not take hold of angels [the fallen angels] — to give them a helping and delivering hand, but He did take hold of [the fallen] descendants of Abraham — to reach them a helping and delivering hand.

Hebrews 2:16

The lake of fire was prepared for the devil and his angels, not for man. (Matthew 25:41.) However, if you choose the devil's ways, you must go where he goes when you leave this life.

I understand why so many women are disillusioned and in so much pain, because I have been there. I do not blame them or the men around them. I blame that state of being *on their not knowing who they are.*

I would say to those women, "Let the oil of healing into your heart by seeking God's Word on all this, and let the Holy Spirit bring peace."

You do not have to take my word for the truths in this book. I have given you the scriptures. Look them up for yourselves. Study the history of the Church and the state of women in Jewish and Greek cultures in the times of the early Church. Separate Paul's writings into categories and see that he was not against women.

Find Out Who You Are

No one can misidentify you or really hinder you, if you already know who you are in Christ.

For years we blamed our failures on a man, or we blamed other women who were jealous, or we blamed it on our denominations — and sometimes they *were* holding us back. However, if we would have gotten in the Word and allowed the Spirit of God to tell us who we are, then none of those things would have ever affected us anyway.

Many of us experienced a lot of sickness and pain and hurt and discouragement and by the time we did finally get into our ministries, we were a mess. That is because we would not allow the Word of God to identify who we are in Him.

The foundational scripture of Ephesians 2:10 proves that God has a plan for all His children, male and female. Our destiny was prepared for us even from before the foundation of the world.

Ephesians 2:10, one of my favorite verses, is a scripture, ladies, that you should know from the depths of your heart if God has called you to minister. That scripture will unlock revelation to you as never before and literally set you free as it did me.

The works preordained for us were not just any kind of works but *good* works, works of excellence, works that were in His mind from before the foundation of the world. They were predestined.

The Amplified Version calls them pre-planned before you ever came into the earth.

One thing I do know is that more and more today we are seeing that God is using females in every aspect of ministry, regardless of who likes it and who does not. Apparently, God likes it!

Not long ago, a certain very large denomination ruled that women could be ministers but no longer serve in the capacity of pastors.

People began to ask me, "Are you going to pray?" I answered, "No, I am not going to waste my time praying." Why would I pray? The Bible never said "the violent" take denominations by force. We are not the violent. God has already given us the Kingdom. (Matthew 11:12.)

I am militant enough to stand because no one can legislate my calling away or demote me. Also, no Christian is chained to that denomination. All a woman pastor has to do is allow God to show her the doors that He desires for her to go through to fulfill the call upon her life. You watch God work for her when she is militant enough to go through them.

So why would I waste my time praying about that? The denomination's decision is God's business, not mine. I have more urgent things that *are* my business to pray about. The only thing I should be praying for is that those persons who came up against God in this matter will not drop dead!

I pray that God's mercy will come upon those who do not yet know better. However, it would be praying against God to pray His mercy on those who know better and are hardheaded or too intimidated to stand up for the truth.

Do you remember that God told the prophet Samuel, who had loved King Saul, to stop mourning for him because Saul had rebelled against God?

And Samuel came no more to see Saul to the day of his death, but Samuel grieved over Saul; and the Lord repented that he had made Saul king over Israel. The Lord said to

Samuel, How long will you mourn for Saul, seeing I have rejected him from reigning over Israel?...

1 Samuel 15:35, 16:1

Just like Saul, who also had the right to choose, men have had the right to choose to see truth about women in ministry and follow God. Down through the centuries, many have chosen wrongly in the Church.

In other words, men and many women in the Church have adopted wrong doctrines about women and have narrowed God's Kingdom into "small worlds" for them in ministry. However, God is using women now anyway. The Spirit of God is anointing us in every area, and I am so grateful.

Sometimes I am asked to minister on this subject: "Are Females Different Than Males in Ministry?" Basically, I preach what you will find in this book, because the Lord has shown me that first of all we serve spiritually and then we serve naturally.

However, men and women often minister differently. You may ask why this is, if there is no distinction in the Body between genders. There is no distinction in God's eyes or in where He uses male and female. There *are* differences in the natural, just as no two people are alike in the natural.

However, there are two problems in the natural: 1) our souls, that are programmed with artificial differences and 2) our bodies, inherited from Adam with natural gender differences.

Soul gender differences are made up mostly of wrong ideas and society's traditions of how men and women are supposed to be as well as those of religion. These can be changed, just as wrong ideas about the roles of men and women in the Church can be changed.

Body gender differences cannot be changed, but we can learn to understand one another, compromise on things sometimes, and overcome other characteristics by choosing not to act on them — *if* they are causing trouble at home or in the ministry. All we have to do is rightly divide the word of truth by being led by the Spirit of truth. The Spirit of God does His job in us very well!

11

Soul Differences Can Be Changed

Do not be conformed to this world — this age, fashioned after and adapted to its external, superficial customs. But be transformed (changed) by the [entire] renewal of your mind — by its new ideals and its new attitude. . . .

Romans 12:2

God is raising up males *and* females who know what God's Word really says, and we are getting ready to walk together as one. The Body is going to be complete very, very soon. So it does not matter what anyone says. God is going to have His way, always has and always will, although it may look to us as if it takes a long time for His will to be accomplished.

However, there is no time with God, and no one is big enough or bad enough to box with God and win. The Spirit is anointing us in every area we will let Him. He is using women not only in the various helps ministries within the church, but also in the governmental positions of apostles, prophets, evangelists, pastors, and teachers.

What is happening now, I believe, is that the world's thinking is getting so far away from biblical truth that many Christians are seeing that their own minds need renewing in several different areas. The dark is getting darker and the light lighter, and it is becoming impossible to compromise.

Paul wrote to the Romans not to be conformed to the world. Yet all these centuries, where women in ministry are concerned, the Church has been conformed to the world. The apostle called the world's customs and traditions "superficial" because they are temporary and have no spiritual depth.

When we become born again, we are supposed to be transformed by the *entire* renewal of our minds, not just some renewal or partly renewed, but all of our thinking. Then Paul went on to tell us why it was necessary to have new ideals and new attitudes.

. . . So that you may prove [for yourselves] what is the good and acceptable and perfect will of God, even the thing which is good and acceptable and perfect [in His sight for you].

Romans 12:2

For a lot of years I was limited in my thinking, so I understand those who still are. However, I do not have to let them limit me any longer.

I used to say, "I can see that women can hold the first four Church offices, but I cannot see that women can be apostles, Father."

Then God said, "You have just begun to study. I have given you the anointing to go into the Word and study. Get in there and study that out for yourself."

I did that and found all of the things already set out in this book about tenses, genders, and God's original design. I found out that God used women in all of the essential gift positions of governmental authority.

The Word was enough for me. I am not looking for a title. I just know that when God has called you to an office and you accept the call, you are going to be doing the work of that office whether you ever use the "title" or not.

What is in a title? Some people have titles who are not called. Some men pastor churches as a career. They are neither called nor anointed. So what difference does a "label" make? Some pastors' wives do more "pastoring," more caring for the sheep, than the husbands do.

However, we need to look at the gender differences in the natural to see if women and men pastor differently. It is very important to understand two things:

1. There are no differences in the spirit realm between genders. In the Kingdom, the Church, or the Body of Christ — whichever one you call God's people under the New Covenant — there are no longer distinctions between male and female.

2. In the natural world, however, men and women are not alike. There *are* gender differences pertaining to characteristics, not rank, in this earth.

All of the problems of the past centuries concerning women have stemmed from confusing these two issues, these two realms, and from not understanding God's original purpose in creating mankind.

We have looked at this question from a spiritual perspective. Now we need to look at it from a natural perspective.

Why Do Our Minds Need Renewing?

God is bringing us back to the original plan in the garden of Eden before the fall: male and female, walking together and having dominion. When we achieve the kind of unity the disciples and followers of Jesus had on the Day of Pentecost, the Body of Christ is going to go forth in all of His power.

However, there is also a natural part of us, because in the natural, God did separate *adam* into male and female with uniquely different natures. I am referring to human natures, not the nature of God in us as newborn Christians.

Our spirits have the nature of God in us. The scripture that proves that is First John 3:9, which says those born of God cannot practice sin because **the divine sperm, remains permanently within** us. Therefore, the nature of God in our spirits is one thing, but the nature we have formed in our souls can be opposed to

God's nature in us as new creatures. We are spirits who live in bodies and who have souls (minds, wills, and emotions).

Our spirits, the real people we are who will step out of these bodies at death, have been made totally new in Christ. That is *past tense*, because the work was done at the cross about 2,000 years ago. It does not occur when we are born again. What occurs in us at conversion is the result of our accepting what was done two millennia ago.

Our bodies *will* (future tense) be made new at the Resurrection.

Our souls are the *present tense* stage of salvation. God could legally give us new spirits because they were dead as a result of the sin of Adam and Eve. When Jesus died on the cross, the penalty for mankind's disobedience as a race was atoned for, and when we receive that atonement, our own sins also are forgiven.

However, our minds are our own, formed individually by:

*Our reactions to people, places, and things around us

*Information we take in from our homes, schools, and the media

*Our choices of what to file away as truth

*How we choose to react to what happens to us.

In other words, we are born into this world as dead spirits in live bodies because of *adam*, male and female, and through no fault of our own. Therefore, God can give us recreated, alive spirits because of Jesus. In Adam, all sinned; in Jesus, the Second Man, all are made alive.

> **For since [it was] through a man that death [came into the world, it is] also through a Man that the resurrection of the dead [has come]. For just as [because of union of nature] in Adam all people die, so also [by virtue of their union of nature] shall all people in Christ be made alive.**
>
> **1 Corinthians 15:21,22**

All we do is accept Jesus' death in our place as a free gift.

However, *we* are responsible for our souls, not Adam and Eve, not our parents, and not any other person. Therefore, since we chose our own pattern of the Adamic nature, so to speak, we must *choose* to allow those natures to be renewed.

God will not override our wills and do it for us. We must let go of the "old man" (the Adamic nature) and put on "the new man" (the image of Christ within us). (Ephesians 4:22.) If God were going to override the right to choose that He built into mankind, He would make everyone get saved!

> **The Lord does not delay and be tardy or slow about what He promises, according to some people's conception of slowness, but He is long-suffering (extraordinarily patient) toward you, *not desiring that any should perish*, but that all should turn to repentance.**
>
> **2 Peter 3:9**

Babies are born with "clean slates," so to speak. They have live bodies but dead spirits, and they have souls ready to soak up any information that comes along. Yes, parents and teachers and those who bring you up "shape" your world. However, your choices determine what you retain of all that when you grow up.

It would be nice, of course, if God would replace our old ways of thinking instantly and automatically as He replaces our old spirits. However, Paul made it very clear that *we* must make right choices and replace old thinking, false information, with truth. (1 Corinthians 5:7,8; Colossians 3:9.)

To do that, you must know the Word of God. How can you replace wrong if you do not know what is right? My years of study on this question of women in ministry have included a series of choices to replace falsehoods with truths as God showed them to me. You must renew your mind the same way. There is no shortcut.

God would not tell us to cast off the old nature and renew our minds, if we did not have some lower nature still operating after we are saved, would He?

12

Natural Differences Cannot Be Changed

May Christ through your faith [actually] dwell — settle down, abide, make His permanent home — in your hearts! May you be rooted deep in love and founded securely on love.

Ephesians 3:17

Even in God's work, it is not possible in a fallen world to serve Him directly out of our spirits. His Word is presented to the people filtered through our personalities. When we serve in ministry, we still have our flesh to contend with.

Our minds can be renewed to spiritual thinking, or we can be "soulish." If we still have trouble with lusts of the flesh, we can even minister carnally. In the past fifteen years, we have seen very sad examples of men who ministered that way until God pulled the rug out from under them.

Males and females *often* think and act differently, because of different natures that stem from physical differences. If you have a husband or a wife you know that. We think differently. We do not even communicate the same.

I could say something to my husband, and when he repeats it back to me, it might be totally different from what I said. Yet he looked right at my mouth when I said it.

He could say something to me, and I might think of something totally different than what he meant. We use the same words, but

101

they do not always mean the same thing to both of us. If you do not know that, you can have some trouble in your marriage.

This is so important that I teach communication skills in marriage counseling. In premarital counseling, we talk, then I ask, "What did you hear me say?"

Many times, when they repeat it, I have to say, "No, that is not what I said."

That difference spills over into ministry. God said we must be aware of this problem, so that we can make our leadership decisions in the Spirit only. We cannot make quality decisions when we are ministering according to the way a woman thinks or according to the way a man thinks *because God thinks totally different*. His ways are higher than our ways. (Isaiah 55:9.)

There is not space in this book to go into all the details about the differences in male and female human natures. However, scientific studies have proven that the gender differences in the male and female begin in the womb.

We may have shaped our souls by our choices of what to believe and how to react, but apparently, we had nothing to do with the male/female gender differences. Biological and chemical differences take place in the development of the brain which causes us sometimes to be different in our thought processes.

We can be Holy Ghost-filled and still be incompatible or disagree, if we do not stay in the Spirit *because our thought patterns are different*. Science declares that each gender accesses different sides of the brain. That affects the way we first respond to things.

If we respond on the side of our brain that is more emotional, which women normally do, then we will respond emotionally if we are not in the Spirit. To men, if they are not careful, everything is objective with no feelings involved.

That is why sometimes when we have male pastors, we may think they are cold and indifferent. Or when we have female pastors, we may think they are emotional. We need to be led by the

Spirit in our leadership decisions. We must consider the fact that we do not serve in our ministries as spirit beings only, but also serve in our natural personalities and nature.

It seems to me that a female leader has to be more cautious in leadership, and not just because of gender bias against us. We ought to be cautious because we have a tendency to be led more by emotions.

Something very important to remember along this line is this: *Not every male or female will necessarily fall into these same categories exactly alike all the time.* I have known men who think with their emotions (subjectively) and women who think logically. Generally speaking, however, by and large, men and women are different in nature.

We do not have to apologize for our created differences. We just need to rely on the Holy Spirit to "translate" what the other sex is really saying.

Every generality may not pertain to every reader in every area. You may not fall into every category. All I am saying is that, in general, we act according to these differences until and unless we are Spirit-led.

General Male/Female Characteristics

Normally, males are willing to take risks more than females. They will venture out and take a gamble quicker than a woman would. Females a lot of times are more cautious. We have more foresight. We tap into spiritual things a lot easier, so we are on guard a little more. We do not usually make decisions quickly.

Males tend to be more logical. They look for facts.

Females look for explanations. That is why when wives talk and want to explain something, we tend to go into these long explanations or conversations with our husbands.

Ladies, let me give you a word of caution. First of all, if you talk too long about something men are not interested in, they will shut you out and not even hear you. They learn to do that very early as little boys, especially if their mothers tend to "go on and on" about things.

Then they think wives or other women in their adult lives are doing the same thing. If you say more than three sentences in a row, they literally may not hear you. You will find that you are just talking to yourself, and then you get mad.

On the other hand, women have more intuition, more awareness. We are more alert to what is going on around us. We like to understand things, so we need more information. Men just want to know "what," not "how, when, and where."

Males are usually a little more impersonal, more business-minded. Females have a tendency to be more personal, more intimate, more tenderhearted. I am not saying this is the way it is across the board, but it is usually the way we are. Why? It is because females are nurturers by created nature.

Therefore, if you have a male pastor and wonder why he is not getting all emotional over things, it is because that is not his nature. If you know this, you will not take it personally.

Men have a tendency to neglect things at times. They are more forgetful and more thoughtless about certain things because their minds are preoccupied with other things women might not think as important.

Women may keep up with details better, but we have a tendency to complain about things more. We have more of a need to express our feelings. If a husband does not want to know how his wife feels about something, she more than likely will think he does not care.

If we have to hold something in, it can be like a time bomb going off. There is going to be some trouble later on if we cannot talk about it. A lot of times women end up telling acquaintances or even strangers their business, because they have to talk to someone.

"Someone, listen! Someone, pay attention before I go crazy here! Ah, I got to let this out."

We want to share what we think and feel, while men are more practical and keep their feelings to themselves.

Men are more future-minded, more goal-oriented, while women are usually more present-minded. We are not worried about painting walls tomorrow. We want them painted now, today!

"This wall needs to be painted now. What do you mean we have to wait till next week to get the paint? We are going to the store right now and get the paint. I know exactly the color."

Males by nature are usually initiators. Women, on the other hand, a lot of times are responders. We do not like to be the one to start things.

It is not female nature to leave things unfinished. We do not like "loose ends." So I usually keep an eye on the women in our church. If they seem very unorganized, I know there is some emotional stuff going on that needs to be dealt with, because that is not a normal woman's nature.

Men are usually more consistent, more regular, more apt to do things the same way and do not "go with the flow" easily.

Women adapt more. It is easier for us to go with change. Women are not so apt to think because we have done it the same way for years, it is sacred and cannot be changed.

A lot of times, while our husbands are asleep, we are thinking. Home is a husband's escape, a place to rest, relax, and recoup. Home for wives many times is a base of operations, a place to start from, a place to make plans.

That is why you find a lot of women in ministry get projects done quickly, because we think that thing out and then are ready to go.

"Get a group of workers together. Let's get together and take care of this problem. I do not care if we stay here all night long. This sanctuary is going to be painted tonight! We are not waiting to do part of it tomorrow."

The communication of men usually is to the point, straightforward, while our communication is more sensitive and roundabout. We listen and observe a little longer.

Men are starters and more aggressive. Women are usually more submissive, more willing to let someone else lead. Oddly enough, women are more in charge in the spirit realm than in the natural. We are fighters. We are warriors in the spirit realm, and we want to go in and just kill the devil with everything in us.

In the natural, however, if we are not careful, we can live lives of bondage because we are quick to take the blame, even when it is not fair. We just want things to be okay. Sometimes, we want a relationship so much that we keep taking unfairness, injustice, and even abuse. Then we wonder why God is not doing anything about our situations.

He is not going to, because then He would be making choices for you. You have to get out of the flesh and over in the spirit realm and bind the devil or leave the situation.

Take Charge of Your Nature

Women can go on living in abusive situations, calling it "submission" and live miserable lives. They do not realize we are the sons of God and we ought to have all of the good life God promised us. However, for some reason, some of us think that being submissive is the same thing as being "a doormat."

I am not talking about usurping authority in the natural, but on understanding who you are in the natural and in Christ. God said we ought to walk according to who He created us to be. In order for the whole body to be blessed, we need to identify who we really are and say, "Okay, closure to this thing right here."

Men have a tendency to be more egoistical, more prideful. A lot of men are more conscious of self than are women. It happened in the very beginning in the garden, and it has not ended yet.

Women have a tendency to be more jealous and covetous of one another. Men are more apt to be competitive with one another but not jealous.

If another woman comes into church with a new dress on, we have a tendency to begin looking at her funny.

"Where did she get the money for that dress? She does not have extra money. She has been running up her credit cards."

Perhaps someone gave her the dress, but we do not normally think first of that possibility. Even if we compliment her, we may not be thinking complimentary thoughts!

Or if someone puts on a little weight, the first thing someone will say is, "Are you gaining weight?"

Now does she need to hear you say that? Do you think she does not know that? Does she need to hear negative things? Perhaps the person has gained weight because she is depressed. Commenting on the obvious fact only makes her more depressed.

We do not need to greet one another in that way. You do not need to ask someone how long since she had her hair done, for example. If you think her hair needs to be done, make an appointment and send her to the best hairdresser in town.

If you cannot do that, simply do not say anything. Be quiet.

Ladies, we need to watch those negative tendencies. That is a strong characteristic. I am not saying no man is ever jealous, but for women there is a tendency. We ought to be so careful to walk in love, not human nature.

We covet things. We do not want to wait until our season. We want it right now because Mary got it and Sue got it, so we want it right now. That is why a lot of women are in debt, especially in ministry. In the early seasons in ministry, it is easy to think you have to have the same designer suits as someone else in ministry.

The fact is that you cannot afford them. Live honestly before the Lord. Take the same dress and get a different scarf or some different earrings and a different pair of shoes. You can wear the same dress and no one will know. In your season, you will be able to buy clothes and enjoy them more, because you will not have to finish paying for something twelve years later that is worn out and gone.

First of all, in order to get rid of that kind of thinking, you have to like yourself. To do that, you must know beyond the shadow of a doubt that you are very important to God just the way you are. He does not have another child like you. There are some things we can enhance about ourselves. However, we must learn to like ourselves just as we are.

Males need self-esteem, to feel worthwhile. That is why the Bible tells a wife to respect and esteem her husband. That is why you find a lot of men have a hard time with women who are anointed in ministry because they want the limelight, so you are a threat.

Where we are jealous, they need to feel important. Both are characteristics of the Adamic nature still influencing us although we have recreated spirits. We still act like who we were. Females need security, assurance, and protection so much that we will put up with anything to have someone like us. If we would just act ourselves, people will like us.

In a nutshell, men get affirmed as worthwhile because of what they do; women, because of who they are as reflected in those they care about. Therefore, men are more task-oriented or work-directed, where women are people-oriented. Often, there will be more social events in a church pastored by a woman.

The last general gender difference I want to mention is that, believe it or not, men are defeated by discouragement more often than women. Men are easy to be dismayed. On the other hand, women are defeated by loneliness and lack of companionship.

That is why it is hard for a woman to be successful in marriage and ministry. We tend to let that "lonely syndrome" keep us from going into the fullness of who God created us to be.

The answer to these gender differences is found in Paul's words to the Christians at Ephesus quoted at the beginning of this chapter. (Ephesians 2:17.) If through faith, we allow Christ to make His permanent home in our hearts, we will be rooted in love and founded on love, and we can love one another as Jesus loved us.

The Bible tells of several women of influence who were accepted by men and who operated in love.

13

Biblical Women of Influence

Now Deborah, a prophetess, the wife of Lappidoth, judged Israel at that time . . . under the palm tree of Deborah . . . in the hill country of Ephraim; and the Israelites came up to her for judgment.

Judges 4:4,5

The Bible gives many examples of women who provided godly leadership, if we need an Old Testament precedent for God allowing women in ministry. Deborah is one who was set by God as a judge, a prophetess, and a leader in Israel.

She was able to tell Israel's General Barak what God had said to her. Barak then declared that he would not go to battle without her. (Judges 4:4-8.)

Deborah was a woman. She was also a wife who knew where to be, when to be there, and who to follow. She stayed with God right up until the end. She acted as a general in that battle, and Barak lost credit for not being willing to go without her.

The background is this: Israel did evil in the sight of the Lord once again in the days when "every man did what was right in his own eyes" before kings were set over the nation. (Judges 17:6.) When the people did evil, God allowed their enemies to oppress them.

God raised up military champions in those days to throw off the yoke of bondage that had come upon the people and to restore the nation of Israel to pure worship of Him.

111

A judge, which is not exactly the translation of what they were called, carried the title or walked in the anointing of a ruler. They were known as deliverers, spiritual and political leaders, and also as "saviors," or one who saves. The judges portrayed the role of Christ, or "imaged" the role of Christ as Savior of God's people.

First, the judges would deliver the people and then rule and administer justice. God showed me that, actually, the judges were very much like our present-day pastors, with the addition of being warriors as well.

Deborah was a Spirit-led, multi-gifted woman who filled a combination of offices.

She walked in the office of prophet.

She walked in the office of a judge.

She was a psalmist, and she was also a military leader. The woman was a warrior from her heart. No other judge except Samuel fulfilled the role of both prophet and judge but Deborah.

Her authority under God was evidenced by Barak, the military leader who hesitated to lead the armies of Israel out to war without receiving her guidance as well as her presence.

There were eleven men and one woman who ruled part or all of Israel for various periods of time during some 350 years between the conquest of Canaan and the anointing of Saul as first king.

The judge before Deborah was named Ehud. After he died, the children of Israel slid into idol worship and other evils again, so **the Lord sold them into the hand of Jabin king of Canaan . . .** (Judges 4:2). Who sold them? It could not be any plainer that the Lord did it.

The commander of Jabin's army was a man named Sisera, apparently much feared by the Israelites.

Barak said to Deborah, "If you will go with me, then I will go, but if you won't go with me, then I won't go." (Judges 4:8.)

And she said, I will surely go with you; nevertheless, the trip you take will not be for your glory; for the Lord will sell Sisera into the hand of a woman. And Deborah arose and went with Barak to Kedesh.

Judges 4:9

He knew that having Deborah with him would assure the army of God's divine presence. Her spiritual, apostolic, and prophetic authority were given to her by God. I believe Deborah's real effectiveness was her spiritual commitment and her walk with God that made her able to hear Him.

She knew her purpose, and it gave her great power and authority. She knew God as El Elyon.[1] She knew He was Almighty God in her life. I believe she demonstrated the possibility for today's women to allow the Spirit of God to fill us, to form us, and to rule and reign in our lives to bring us to purpose and destiny.

Deborah Was Called in Her Own Right

God would have given her a husband who would have gone to that battle if He had wanted a man to do it.

Was God ignorant?

Did He not know her husband before she married him?

Did He not know one of Israel's generals would fear to go to battle unless He had an anointed person with Him?

When did God find out His called and anointed woman was going to be a warrior at heart? He knew that before the foundation of the world. God called Deborah for the purpose for which He used her, not to fill in for someone else.

He did not use her because Barak would not go without her, or in place of Barak, or in place of her husband. He used her because she was the female *adam* He knew would serve His purpose at that time and place.

According to Numbers 11:25, the prophetic gift has its source in the Spirit of the Lord. Therefore, the prophet or the prophetess is actually a spokesman of God and for God. Moses' sister Miriam was the very first prophetess of whom we have a record who praised God before all of the people (Exodus 15:20), but Deborah was not like Miriam. Deborah was different.

The objective Spirit of Deborah's God elevated her above her people and above heroes before and after her. No man looked down on her. In fact, they celebrated her victory. They recognized the anointing on her life. That is what should matter, the anointing.

At that time in the history of Israel, women were given respect when called by God. You will find over and over that certain women from Miriam to Esther, who lived in Persia after the exile, were accepted as equals in the nation.

The role of women deteriorated during the Jews' seventy-year exile in Babylon, five centuries before Jesus.

I believe that in these last days of God's outpouring of His Spirit, many Baraks will say to their Deborahs that they will not go to battle without them — and it will not be out of order.

I feel now is the timing of God to restore men and women back to divine order in the home and in the Kingdom of God.

I believe they will walk together as one under God's mandate to "tend the garden" of God, to multiply, to take dominion over every living thing, and as the bride of Christ, to prepare for His coming.

It is the hour for men and women to come to faith and stop living under the doctrine of the Adamic nature that takes God's plan of authority for marriage and applies it across the board to all situations involving men and women.

Modern Deborahs must stop allowing themselves to be given the status of children and begin to walk in the maturity of sons.

[1]Strong's "Hebrew Dictionary," #5945. *El Elyon* means "an elevation, lofty, high, uppermost," or as a title, "The Supreme."

14

Are We Children or Sons?

But now that the faith has come, we are no longer under a trainer — the guardian of our childhood. For in Christ Jesus you are all sons of God through faith.

Galatians 3:25,26

The King James Version of the Bible translates Galatians 3:26 as we are all **children of God.** The word translated in most other versions as "sons" is the Greek *huios*.[1] The Greek word whose primary meaning is "child" is *brephos*,[2] denoting "a young child, an infant, a babe."

If someone can just call you a child of God or a daughter of the Lord, then they can kind of keep you separated from all of the benefits of God. However, when rightly dividing the Word of truth (2 Timothy 2:15), "sons" are mature. "Children" are under age, needing a guardian. They are to be looked after, not given assignments.

Galatians 3:27 says:

For as many [of you] as were baptized into Christ — into a spiritual union and communion with Christ, the Anointed One, the Messiah — have put on (clothed yourselves with) Christ.

What was Paul talking about? He was saying that, when you become born again, you did not clothe yourself with *Jesus*. You clothed yourself with *Christ*. Your spirit man has been clothed, or covered with, the Anointed One.

117

The last verse of that chapter adds *if we belong to Christ*, the Messiah, and are in Him, then we also are Abraham's offspring (sons) and heirs according to the promise.

What was the promise? The promise given to Abraham of the Spirit of God, the promise of the fullness of God. *Sons of God* means preeminent moral character. It means those who show maturity and a likeness of God's character in Christ.

Those who have put on Christ are actually reflecting the image of God in the earth. That is why different words were used between children of God and sons of God. When you are a child of God, you still need a tutor.

You have not come into the fullness of your inheritance. When you become a son of God, you actually are able to walk in His character, His maturity. You are able to walk in dominion, irre-spective of gender.

Jesus came into the earth for this purpose: *to destroy all the works of Satan* (1 John 3:8). Among the works of Satan was to erase from mankind's memory the image of God or even that there is a God.

Jesus, the man child, came into being for the sole purpose of showing the world what Christ, the Anointed Only Begotten Son of God, looks like in human form. Jesus is the image of man who also was Christ, the image of God. Being all man and at the same time all God is one of the mysteries of the faith.

The word *image* does not mean a statue. It means the essence of being. Jesus took on the essence of God's being as He demon-strated the Christ. That is why He did not do any miracles until He was anointed, until the image of God came upon Him during His visit to John the Baptist's meeting. (Matthew 3:16,17.)

The Apostle John wrote:

> **And the Word was made flesh, and dwelt among us, (and we beheld his glory, the glory as of the only begotten of the Father,) full of grace and truth.**
>
> **John 1:14** KJV

Where did this glory come from? The glory is the essence of God or everything that makes God Who He is. The glory came from the Father, the image of God on Jesus. It was such glory as an only begotten son receives from his father, full of grace (favor, loving-kindness) and truth.

The same glory that the Father gave Him in John 1:14 is the same glory He has now given us. No more, no less. That is why when people say Jesus had the fullness of the Spirit in Him and then they say we have a portion, they are wrong. That is not scriptural.

Who Has the Fullness of the Godhead?

Who has the fullness of the Godhead? Jesus, the Christ, *and* His Body, according to Scripture. We also have the *fullness* of the Godhead. Can we know that for certain? Look at Colossians 1:15,19:

> **[Now] He is the exact likeness** (the image) **of the unseen God — the visible representation of the invisible; He is the First-born — of all creation . . . For it has pleased [the Father] that all the divine fullness — the sum total of the divine perfection, powers and attributes — should dwell in Him permanently.**

There is no question that Jesus is "the exact likeness" of God and has the fullness of God in Him. But what about us? Look at Colossians 2:10:

> **And you are in Him, made full and have come to fullness of life — in Christ you too are filled with the Godhead: Father, Son and Holy Spirit, and reach full spiritual stature. And He is the Head of all rule and authority — of every angelic principality and power.**

It could not be any plainer: **In Christ, you too are filled with the Godhead.** That means with the glory of God as well.

When God recreated each one of us, He recreated us in His image and in His likeness. That also is the image of Christ, the

Anointed One. That is why the Bible never calls us the Body of Jesus, only the Body of Christ.

That is how we can be sons of God. Jesus was the First-born, the Bible says. If He was the first, then there have to be more to follow the first, and there was: Us.

God always has been looking for sons. The first *adam*, male and female, failed through disobedience. Being a very thrifty God who never fails, He "salvaged" the sons of the first man through the sacrifice of the Second, and Last, Man, Jesus.

Now the sons, male and female, make up the Body of Christ.

All of this was a mystery to the children of God under the Old Covenant — and they *were* "children," not yet sons. Paul wrote that the Law was not even a tutor but a servant who led the children from home to the school or to the tutor's house.

There could be no real mature sons, no matter how much the heroes and heroines of faith believed and trusted God (Hebrews 11), until Jesus came as the Messiah, the Christ. Paul wrote to the Colossians about this mystery:

> **The mystery of which was hidden for ages and generations (from angels and men), but is now revealed to His holy people (the saints), to whom God was pleased to make known how great for the Gentiles are the riches of the glory of this mystery, which is, Christ within and among you the hope of [realizing] the glory.**
>
> **Colossians 1:26,27**

Where is the power of God?

Where is the essence of God?

Where is the glory of God? Paul said it is within us, all of us.

How in the world can the power and the glory and the essence of God be in me, yet I cannot teach, I cannot preach, I am not equal, I am subservient to the male *adam* in ministry?

The mystery uncovered was Christ the Anointed One, and His anointing within and among those born again who have the hope, or the earnest expectation, of actually manifesting that glory. God expects us to manifest His glory.

> **Him we preach and proclaim, warning and admonishing every one and instructing every one in all wisdom, [in comprehensive insight into the ways and purposes of God], that we may present every person mature — full-grown, fully initiated, complete and perfect — in Christ, the Anointed One.**

> **Colossians 1:28**

Where is that anointing? It is in us. It is in me. We have it already. Therefore, when we serve God in ministry, whether male or female, God looks for Christ in us, the hope of glory.

So we ought to be able to decree every single day that we have been crucified with Christ so that it is no longer you and I who live but Christ, the glory, the anointing. (Galatians 2:20.)

You ought to start liking yourself because you represent the image, the glory of God. In the things of the Spirit, there is not any more distinction between any of God's sons. We are all one, equally the same in His body, because we belong to the Anointed One. He has come to live in us.

We have inherited the same promises that He promised Abraham. God said from the very beginning, before the fall, that He was going to make all of mankind in His image and likeness.

He said in the very beginning that both male and female alike would have complete authority.

He said in the very beginning they would have an authority over creation.

He said in the very beginning that both would have dominion.

He sent His Son to purchase us out of slavery, out of the bondage of sin and restore us to man's original place in God. God is not going to plan anything and not have it fulfilled.

Commit To Become One

Now look again at one of the verses with which I began this book:

So that they all may be one [just] as You, Father, are in Me and I in You, that they also may be one in Us, so that the world may believe and be convinced that You have sent Me.

John 17:21

There *is* still bias in the churches of America, in spite of all that the Holy Spirit inspired the apostles to write about oneness in the New Testament. However, the only way prejudice can affect you and me is if we allow it to affect us.

We are not literally acting as one, as Jesus prayed. However, holding grudges against those who reject you does not help matters at all.

If someone has closed a door to you, first of all, that was not a door God wanted open anyway. The Bible says God opens doors, and no one can close them, and when God closes doors, no one can open them. (Revelation 3:7.)

A lot of denominational doors closed to me when I first went into the ministry. God showed me first of all that He closed those doors in order to turn me to a people who were walking in the same direction in which He was leading me.

If He had not closed those doors, I would have "gone back to Egypt," because we like familiarity. We like comfort. We like to stay around people who know us and whom we like.

So sometimes God will close a door, and you will think people are rejecting you. They may be rejecting you, but it is in God's plan. Those who reject you will not or cannot go with you, and they will only hinder you.

At that time, I felt as if I was in a season of loneliness. However, God told me that was not loneliness. He had me in a cave, from which He was getting ready to bring me forth. He had to clean up everything in my mind. He had to get rid of all preconceived ideas. He had to get rid of the self-pity.

I thought I was lonely and rejected, because no one cared about me anymore. Actually, I was feeling sorry for myself. After all, I had spent time in so many churches blessing people. I had stayed up all night praying some of them through. I ministered to their marriages, prayed, and prophesied over them.

Now those people had rejected me. I spent some time trying to cry, until God told me to shut up and grow up. If you think God will not tell you to shut up, you are wrong!

He said, "Shut up, and grow up. Then go forth and fulfill that which I have called you to do."

I am sure I am not the only one who has experienced this, because it is time for the sons of God to take their God-given places within His Body, male and female alike, through Christ Jesus.

It is time to cast down the intimidation.

It is time to go forward in the anointing that Christ has provided for the entire body.

It is time for us to truly begin to love one another in the Body: all races and nationalities, both genders, and all social classes.

It is time to show the world that Jesus lives in us, the Light of the world, and is the fullness of the Godhead sitting in Heaven at the right hand of the Father.

I pray that every reader will come into the knowledge of this truth: There are *no* distinctions in the Body of Christ, the Church. Also, I would pray that everyone begins to walk in Colossians 2:6,7:

As you have therefore received the Christ, [even] Jesus

the Lord, [so] walk — regulate your lives and conduct your-selves — in union with and conformity to Him. Have the roots [of your being] firmly and deeply planted [in Him] — fixed and founded in Him — being continually built up in Him, becoming increasingly more confirmed and estab-lished in the faith, just as you were taught, and abounding and overflowing in it with thanksgiving.

As the subject of male and female both being *adam* and all of the consequences of that fact — which are opposite to what is commonly believed — is fairly new to most people, I have added a summary of the most important points.

---

[1] Strong's "Greek Dictionary," #5207.
[2] Ibid, #1025.

Summary

One:

God created man, *adam*, as one being, then separated that being into two genders, male and female. He gave them equal dominion over the work of His hands on this earth and over all the living creatures.

Two:

Adam and Eve forfeited their dominion to Satan, who then became "prince of this world (order)" (John 12:31), which means of all this world's systems — economic, political, social, scientific, and so forth. God never gave man ownership of the earth, so the planet itself remained under God's dominion directly. (Psalm 50:12.)

Three:

Jesus reconciled everything back to God, took dominion from Satan and, as God and the Second Man now rules and reigns. However, everything on earth still has not been put under His feet. Satan is still prince of power of the air (Ephesians 2:2), second heavens, and the world order. He is a defeated foe, not yet put in prison.

Four:

Jesus delegated His authority to the Body of Christ, who is to occupy (taking back territory by becoming salt and light in the world) until He returns. Also, He is our eternal High Priest, and every person born again is part of His royal priesthood, male and female.

Five:

In the Body, the Church, there are no more distinctions between races, genders, and social classes as far as God placing someone in a Church office or using him or her in whatever way He chooses. All are called "sons," as individual temples of God, showing forth His glory and, corporately, as *the* Temple of God.

Six:

In the natural, however, there are authority levels, because everyone cannot rule over everyone else. God is a God of order, not confusion.

His angelic hosts apparently are ranked in order of purpose, not in order of one being more important than another. We know this because the devil's cohorts are the same (Ephesians 6:12), and he must have copied God's arrangement.

Only man was created in God's image, so only man can have imagination and creativity. None of the angelic beings have this as far as we can tell. They were created each for a special purpose and can only obey or disobey. Many of Satan's tactics down through the centuries had to be devised in the mind of some human being and used by the enemy.

All God's sons are important in whatever place He chooses to use them. Authority levels are these:

A. The Godhead: Father, Son, Holy Spirit

B. The written Word of God.

C. Man's conscience, when it is trained by the Word and open to the voice of the Spirit.

D. Churches: *Pastors* with elders, deacons, and so forth under them. *Teachers and evangelists* are under which pastor or apostle God sets them under. *Prophets* are under their local pastors, yet can be sent to others as God wills.

Apostles have authority over churches which they have founded or over whom God sets them.

E. Civil Authority, which is over families as well as communities, states, nations, and kingdoms.

F The Family Unit: Husbands are the heads over their own wives, and husbands and wives are over children. However, the bottom line of the apostle's advice on marriages plus God's original plan, seems to say a couple should work as a team and submit to one another. The responsibility for unity in the family and for final decisions, as well as for responsibility for protection and security, rests with the head.